I0149766

Listen, People.

Compassionate listening
and rising from suicide crisis

by Star Ford

Illustrated by Sky Ford and Jeanie Vo

Listen, People. Compassionate listening and rising from suicide crisis

Credits: Illustrations by Sky Ford and Jeanie Vo. Cover by Jeanie Vo.

Publisher: Star Ford Press, Las Vegas, New Mexico

ISBN: 979-8-9875399-0-3

Library of Congress Control Number: 2022924125

First printing: February 2023

Reviews

This book was absolutely incredible! There were so many paragraphs and pages where I found myself crying because what I was reading was putting into words feelings or experiences I've had that it has felt are rarely, if ever, understood by mental health professionals. As someone who has used crisis lines many times, I can definitely attest to how much more helpful Agora has been to me than many professionally staffed crisis lines (which at times have been downright harmful). I feel that the volunteers at Agora have truly helped me to stay alive and to get to a point where I no longer need to call crisis lines very often at all. I am incredibly grateful for this book, and for Agora, and would recommend this book to literally everyone because I feel there is so much written here that we all need as humans in need of connection, regardless of if someone is or isn't interested in mental health. Please read Listen, People!

-AJ

Star Ford has captured the beautiful spirit of the many people who volunteer at Agora and other volunteer helplines across the country. The importance of encouraging volunteerism and community empathy cannot be stressed enough, especially in times when many of us are feeling isolated and anxious about the future. It is an honor to work with so many people who are willing to give their time to selflessly help strangers who are in distress.

- Molly Brack, Clinical Director

Contents

Introduction..7
Listening...9
Agora...28
Trauma...49
Suicide...57
Categories..64
Healing...75
Leadership...87
Autonomy...98
Learning...115
Life force..137
Professionals...149
Social justice...167
Fun...189
Now what?...198

Introduction

This book addresses how people get into crisis, how they can get out of it, and the role of compassionate listening. I examine the function of life crises in individuals and families, and the tepid national response to the rising suicide rate. I also go into theory and techniques for crisis intervention, and include training materials so you can learn ways to help others.

> 50% of the proceeds from sales of this book are going to volunteer crisis centers. Thank you for your donation!

Each of us is a partially revealed, partially hidden spirit on a trajectory towards a manifestation or purpose of some kind, unique to each person. We are more than our jobs, education, roles, accomplishments, and beliefs: we are that trajectory towards purpose; in other words, we are not something – we are just becoming. We do not need to be happy; we just need to move on our own path. But in crisis, we may have no movement, and no becoming. We can feel we are walking dead, a mere tool for someone, or a cog in a machine. What is written here is not from a religion or motivational speaker. I learned it directly from people in crisis, from my experience as a counselor with Agora Crisis Center at the University of New Mexico, where I have talked to hundreds of people in crisis, and saved some lives. They are my teachers. The director, Molly Brack, has been a true servant leader, an excellent teacher, and an inspiration to me and to many others. My motivation to write started with wanting to put her philosophy and practices into words, in hopes that her inspired and effective ways can be spread widely. The Agora approach to suicide and other personal crisis – centered on listening and compassion – seems to be more effective than that of the wider mental health systems.

It may seem like only a certain special kind of person could handle talking with people who are close to death, one after the other. People tell me, "I could never do that!" But it turns out that compassion is learnable. I am a good example of that, as a person who was not a natural at this; Molly's training was able to reach me and nurture a previously hidden and undeveloped ability. Now I am comfortable talking to people about trauma and death.

Listening

LISTENING WITH OR AGAINST

Imagine two immigrants struggling to find work in a new country, and one recounts the troubles and worries about this to the other. Since they are both in the same predicament, the listener might reply with something like the following:

- Yeah, same here.
- It's not fair.
- Ain't that a bitch.

People in the same predicament

Now imagine the person instead recounted the complaint to someone else who was farther away from the situation – someone who is trying to be helpful but is not as able to feel what the situation is like. That person might reply with something like the following:

- I'm sure something will come along eventually.

- Maybe you should take a class.

- Have you tried the vocational rehab office?

This second person is trying to be supportive, and those kinds of responses might actually be good advice, but they are contradictory to the experience being related. They are avoiding acknowledgment of the frustration and other feelings, and it is as if they said, "your feelings are wrong because there is a simple solution." The first type of response is "With" and the second is "Against." It feels adversarial even when the listener is trying to help. With-responses are infinitely more helpful; for people experiencing a problem or crisis, the need to be heard and understood is usually far more acute than the need to determine what to do about it.

You can imagine how the fellow immigrant needed no training in "listening skills" to be able to empathize; it is just natural to be able to empathize when you are in the same boat as someone else. The farther we are away from the experience of someone else though, the less natural those With-responses are, but we can still learn how to just "be with." We can learn to unlearn the complex adversarial responses and be simpler, less wordy, and just say things like "ain't that a bitch."

Ironically it seems the higher up the professional ladder you go, the more likely you are to get Against-responses. Maybe the farther into the helping professions one goes, the more needs to be unlearned to reach the simplicity of just hearing someone.

NAMING FEELINGS

I once was in a small swarm of people surrounding a teen who had a snowboard accident and was in pain. People were all trying to help. He was increasingly amped up as more people were yelling their advice. Someone would say, "where does it hurt?" and he would say, "they must think I'm pathetic," or someone would say, "It's OK, it could happen to anyone!" and he would say, "no, I was being stupid!" Or someone would say, "try to stay still and relax" and he would say, "I need to try that jump again – I know I can do it!" Seeing how the "help" had become so combative, I waited for an opening and said, "You're really frustrated." Almost instantly he became calm and was ready to acknowledge that he needed medical help, and all that argumentative energy in the room came to a halt. He, like many in an emergency situation, needed to be heard first before he needed anything else. The word "frustrated" was offered to him; it was not a word he had said. But he had been trying to express it in different ways, and hearing that word as a summary was the magic that let him know someone understood what it was like for him to fail at something that was so important to him.

LISTENING TO SELF-JUDGMENT

Some of the more difficult personal issues to give a With-response to are those that are self-judging. For example, here is something someone might say on crisis call: *I'm so fat and ugly and everyone hates me. I'll never get a boyfriend.*

Many people, hearing this, would leap to an Against-response, or a contradiction, because it feels insulting to confirm to the caller that she may in fact be fat and that people do not like her. Some habitual Against-responses might be to deny that she is fat, or say that it is OK to be any weight, point out that not literally *everyone* hates her, remind her that she cannot predict the future, give advice on ways to meet people, and so on.

Molly says that a crisis is like the person has fallen into a well, and they can only see darkness. As helpers, we need to go into the well and just be with them there, to affirm how bad it really is for them. A helper can simultaneously be with the person, and also stay outside the hole, in order to stay grounded and see a further horizon than the caller can in the moment.

We can hear the feelings behind the self-judgment and give words to it. We do not know if the person would ever have a boyfriend so we cannot offer false hopes or promises that it would happen. Some ways to reflect honestly without being insulting are to assign feelings to it, like being lonely, sad, or disconnected. We can ask what happens when people hate them, and how it feels. We need to take the view they hold as true as the starting point.

Being with someone in crisis

WHAT TO SAY

The first experiences of listening to a stranger relate horrible stories can leave us at a loss for words. We know we should not judge or offer platitudes, but what can we say? If there is silence, it can feel awkwardly long. But just as a low pressure zone in the atmosphere draws currents towards that space, a low pressure communication technique leaves silence that draws out more truth. We can just say, "go on" or "Can you tell me more about it?"

What if the person is saying things that we doubt are true or that we do not want to support? For example, "My mom wants to kill me" (unlikely) or, "I'm going to get back at him for taking my girl" (unwise). We still listen from inside the perspective they have; it does not imply agreement to listen.

Here is another example situation, after which I will discuss a variety of things that can be said in response.

> Scenario: *The person in crisis has a husband who will not let her see her mother, and is angry if she is not home when he gets home. She is under constant surveillance and isolated. He earns money and she does not. She is calling because she is so lonely and wants to find a way to see mom without making him mad.*

The job of listening is to hear not only the story, but the feelings, the history, and the reasons. We need to understand and feel the trap or predicament that she is in. We are not looking for her way out; we are first trying to get in.

A remarkably powerful starting point is to simply say, "we can talk through that," or "thanks for letting me know the situation." She may not be sure if it is OK to talk about, because perhaps other people have told her she is not allowed to talk, so just acknowledging the situation exists is already helpful. We can also say, "I'm sorry you are going through all that" or, "that sounds very difficult." No matter how tentative they are about how bad it is, we always go with the superlative of acknowledging it as "very difficult." It is not helpful to try to put perspective on it by suggesting that maybe it is not really that bad. This is because they are giving you the gift of trust to hear their dark secrets, which is hard to do, and even if the first thing they start with is not that terrible, it is still connected to the deeper things that are terrible. So by acknowledging that what they are going through is extremely painful, it acknowledges the deeper things that they have not revealed yet.

A second approach is naming feelings or asking about them, as I discussed in the other scenarios. "How does it feel?" is a great question, though is often too generic to start with. If we can hear frustration or loneliness in the tone, we can ask, "It sounds so lonely. Are you feeling frustrated or angry about it?" This way of throwing in a few feeling words allows the person to self-reflect and be more specific. It is fine to guess wrong; maybe in her case she does not feel any anger. Maybe she really loves him and feels a lot of empathy for the stress he seems to be going through. Maybe she fears and loves him at the same time. Suppose in asking about feelings, it comes out that she is loyal and feels shame because he does so much for her and protects her, while she "only" raises the child. Maybe she adds that when they met, she was homeless and in a dangerous situation which he rescued her from. She had run away at 17 because her parents were fighting constantly. We now understand the feelings are complex because the history is complex.

Another kind of response is to show that we have heard by placing the situation in the context of universal values. For example, "No one should have to go through that." Or, "You've been so strong to endure this situation for so long." This type of feedback again acknowledges how bad it is, which lets the caller know they are heard. It has the danger of being a little judgmental, and might feel adversarial if she actually feels weak or that she does deserve it. Usually people appreciate it though.

Finally, we can find out about options. We could ask, "How would it feel to leave him?" A question like that is literally asked to find out how it would feel, not as disguised advice. It could be leading in a way, but it also shows that it is OK to talk about all options. She may say it is out of the question and she may protect him. It may be from a sense of threat and maybe we are even smart enough to connect the fact that her dad was controlling and this is a repeating pattern. But our main job is listening, which means staying within her world as she sees it. (We might actually be clever, but that is not what matters – she knows herself best.)

CRISIS RESPONSE PHASES

While each call is different, there are some phases of an effective crisis call, which are essentially: (1) rapport, (2) development, (3) next steps.

Rapport means establishing basic trust – creating a conversational space that is safe enough for a person in crisis to say personal things. The counselor demonstrates they are hearing them by reiterating or naming feelings. One of the main shifts that happens psychically for a caller in this phase is going from a feeling that the problem is shameful, unique, and hard to talk about, to a feeling that the problem is discrete, identified and named, and acceptable to talk about. It feels like taking hidden things from under a table and placing them on a well-lit tabletop, then being OK with looking at it from all sides.

People call a crisis line when their family and other relationships are lacking in some way – they are not being heard in daily life. So it is so important to listen and demonstrate that we are hearing without judgment. The skill of listening has a lot to do with clearing our conversational approach of judgment and answers and everything else that is not listening. So in a way it is more of a reduction of repertoire, not adding a new technique. When we remove all the non-listening, we tend to say more basic things in response, even as basic as "tell me more" or "that feels sad." Getting to this simple core from the start is important in building rapport and trust.

Development is next, and it is about connecting the thing that we identified and put on the tabletop with other things in life, asking open ended questions, clarifying feelings, or just being quiet while the person gets everything out that they need to say. I often make notes on paper, sometimes even boxes and lines that make a mental map more concrete. This helps me focus and stay in discovery mode. I often feel a sense of honor to be the one to get the inside scoop about someone's life. Often I am the first person to ever hear it, and these bits of information are raw, precious, and vulnerable. We are still avoiding advice or resolution in this phase.

The last phase is about next steps, but importantly, we are still mainly listening. We ask what next steps might be, offering some ideas sparingly if needed.

A more detailed model of this has five phases, and I will get to that later. For now, just reflect on how we can be so helpful by doing *less:* no diagnosis, no advice, maybe not even any shared experience. We do not have to *know* anything; we only have to learn about their life in their own words, let it touch and affect us, and feel it with the person.

CONNECTING THE DOTS

Here is a bit of conversation that introduces a few aspects all together:

> *Life is exhausting. I just can't deal. I mean, I have friends and everything is OK, it's just me that's messed up. My parents are trying to help and I want to make them happy. I just feel like no one knows me. I have a fake smile and they think I'm happy all the time but they don't know.*

As the listener, we could choose to initially attach to exhaustion, or what it means to be "messed up," or feeling unseen. In other words, we could approach each of these parts separately. But also the more we connect the dots into a full picture, the more our feedback helps. In cases like this, it might jump out that the work it takes to maintain a fake smile is a lot of work, and that is why she feels exhausted. Actual conversations may be drawn out with a lot of detours and tangents, and the listener has to be doing analytical work, not just paying attention to the last thing said. Since my memory and attention span can falter, I have to use paper and draw out the mental map, in order to notice what dots can be connected. For the person in crisis, seeing how the fake smile is possibly the cause of other problems could be a big step. We do not advise on what to do about it; just bringing that to light is empowering.

Here is something else a caller might say:

> *My dad has been having more outbursts and I'm constantly thinking he will hit me again, or worse. I've been abused my whole life by different men and I can't take it anymore. I want to find a way to kill myself and dispose of the body so there is nothing left.*

How can we listen to this? First, there are knee-jerk Against-responses, such as: "That's not the answer. You can get through this." That answer would be contradictory and would fail to acknowledge the unstated feelings or needs. The caller may double down and argue their point in order to be heard, or just give up trying to communicate.

Another type of response is just "yeah" or something showing that you are listening without making any summary or judgment about it. This may seem like a non-response but it can be quite helpful because it keeps the caller in focus and keeps the door open to say more. The caller is steering.

If we have been trained in active listening, we might say something that repeats the message back for clarity, such as: "Your dad has outbursts and you are thinking about suicide because of it." This can be helpful, and we can go a lot farther than that.

A deeper kind of active listening is a response like: "That sounds terrifying, not knowing when he will snap." This adds feeling words and pieces together things that were unsaid. A response like this confirms very well that the listener has understood at least a part of it.

And finally, a somewhat more abstracted and even more helpful response could be: "They can never touch you again if you're not there, and that idea brings you peace." This kind of response pulls together everything they said with a high level of compassion and no judgment.

This last response is as if the caller gave some dots on a paper, and the listener connected the dots and drew the whole shape. When we respond in this way, the person in crisis can feel heard in a deeper way. When someone is heard more deeply, it hits a calming button at their core. Many people have said, "Exactly!" or, "You're the first person to understand me!" when I have done this. It turns out that no matter how twisted, impractical, or violent their thoughts may be, being with them in those thoughts is more powerful than providing them with more rational and acceptable thoughts.

ADVICE

Some people ask for advice. Sometimes I have given advice because ultimately it is not about rules; it is two humans in a short-term friendship being natural and as real as possible. But mostly we try to facilitate discovery of the direction to go instead of give direct advice. We can say things like:

- "Let's explore some options – what have you thought about so far?"

- "What would you advise for someone else who was framed?"

- "What would it feel like to confront him about it directly?"

WHY LISTENING WORKS

Being heard is perhaps the most vital ingredient in moving through a sudden crisis like a snowboarding accident, and it is also the most vital ingredient in healing from long-lasting trauma. It develops the voice to be able to talk about things by giving words to those things, and it energizes the power within the person to survive and make changes.

The more someone is heard, the more they will say. Some callers test the waters by telling a small bit of a story, then open up more later after they feel the listener is really listening. As listeners we have to prove that we are not being robotic or scripted, and are really listening. The more inferences we can make about what they omitted and the more summarizing or feeling words we can add, the more we can prove that we really heard.

Another part of the proof of being present is "matching." If we can match the tone and emotional level, we can feel what they are going through more easily, and it makes them more comfortable. It involves a bit of acting so one has to be careful. The technique is used by salespeople to make potential customers feel as if they are talking to someone like them; for example, they shift their accent and posture to mimic the customer. So the technique can be used for deceit, but also consider how actors try to get into the mindset of the characters they play: this helps them really feel compassionately for the characters' struggles.

Compassionate listening is not always soft and gentle – particularly when matching the tone of someone who is animated. If a caller is angry, the listener can affirm the anger by yelling "Damn straight!" and use the actor's technique of getting into that character as a path into really understanding the real person. Some of the Agora volunteers talk about listening by using "Agora" as a verb. For example: "I had to Agora my roommate on the head to get her out of her rut." This is not soft, passive listening; it's more like bonking someone on the head with questions, an active Socratic method of empowering and untangling.

READING AURAS

I am one of the minority of people who usually misses the surface presentation that people expose, and can more easily see the emotions, values, and internal struggles of people. So if for example, someone is trying to hide anger and wearing a fake smile or some other surface social construction, I am usually unable to notice the smile and can only see the anger. It is quite difficult to be this way, because I notice so little of what people look like that I cannot distinguish or recognize them (also called face-blindness, a common aspect of autism), and sometimes cannot remember that someone exists at all. People who know me and expect me to remember them have thought I was extremely rude for ignoring them. This internal-only focus is very isolating, even disabling.

A way in which this way of being has sacrificed a lot of relationships is through seeing more than I am allowed to. People have felt too exposed around me because I sense what they are going through without words, and their efforts to conceal it from me do not work. They might be trying to keep a secret from themselves, but my presence exposes it to them, which can be unsettling. Then some people get angry at me over a sense of violating boundaries, even though I have no choice – it is not something that can be turned off.

Before my crisis counseling training, I was considered cold, aloof, and even severe – certainly not compassionate. Reading auras, as I call that internal-only focus, was not conscious or refined, and I had no way to talk about it. As a child, I did not understand that other people were not like this. What others can do in their 20s took me far into my 40s to be able to do. But through the Agora training and experience, I was able to bring the undeveloped compassion from this to a more conscious level. I can connect the dots from a caller's psychic life map fairly well now, and so many people have said I understood them more than anyone else ever has. Yet I can hardly make friends in normal life. The internal-only focus makes the short-term "relationships" with people in crisis feel natural, and normal relationships often feel unreachable.

After a few years of crisis work, when I now connect two or more dots in an apparent leap, I have learned to trust my intuition and will label it as such. For example, I may say something analytical like: "My intuition is that you are quite sensitive, focused on justice, and very creative, but your mom misses the moral part and believes that the crying is for attention, when it is actually for protection." If I say this after talking with them for only a minute or two, I have gotten a lot of incredulous responses, like, "how did you know that?" The aura reading could seem like the occult to some people, but it is not from any other plane; it just draws on data that they have already given me.

Here is an incident from before my Agora training that helps shed light on internal-only focus. Someone I was starting to get to know told me about an organization she was starting, whose purpose was to help victims of sex trafficking. In the telling I said almost nothing. After talking to me for an hour straight, which for her was like talking to a silent mirror, some fears came to the surface for her. She showed the panic of accidentally revealing too much. I never heard from her again.

Looking back and reconstructing this, I believe that she realized I suspected that she was not only a victim in the past, but that she was reliving the pattern with her boyfriend currently. This is something she probably intended to hide but she "told" me about it between the lines. Then perhaps she got scared she would be seen as a fraud if people knew she was still holding onto it. I knew her motives were pure and that it is hard to get out of the self-oppression, but I did not say that, or say anything at all. She was consciously attempting to talk about the painted over layer – her organization and the needs of the other victims. But she accidentally gave me too much of the whole story, and then possibly got afraid of me exploiting or judging it.

Since then I have learned more about auras. One thing is that it feels dangerous to be so exposed. At that time, I did not understand that most people routinely exploit information they have on others. The intensity of her fear after that hour of listening was baffling back then, but now I can understand the fear better. If it happened now, I would interject more reassurances and be mindful of slowing down instead of bringing up so much trauma so fast. I wish I could have reassured her that it was okay to be incomplete. The second thing I learned is that anything gained from auras can only be used compassionately; if I was intending to exploit, I would not be able to receive the information in the first place. I wish I could have reassured her that her struggles were safe with me.

My development from a cold, more protected person into someone who could help in a crisis had to do with refining the compassion that was buried way in there, and letting it be expressed with some intentional containment. Instead of just absorbing as much and as fast as people unwittingly reveal (thus scaring them away), I learned with the training to expose more of me while respecting others' psychic boundaries better.

Every trained listener probably goes through some process of bringing up and refining their natural compassion, and we all end up being different. No listener is objectively "better at it" than another because the points of contact are different for each person. We are not aiming for uniformity.

LISTENING IN BURSTS OF TIME

Agora listeners usually spend four hours per week (some-times eight) on shift. This limit allows the volunteer to engage vulnerably, make mini-friendships with callers, and come out of that depth for the rest of the week. There is a mental preparation time and a recovery time. Sometimes there is a need for recovery because some contact was diffi-cult, but more often the recovery is just because so much energy was exchanged. I do not necessarily feel drained after – I may even feel energized – but either way it is an intensity that cannot be maintained every day. Of course some days I am not as engaged and may only be a little helpful or neutral. One cannot expect to be an aura-reading master of connecting the dots every week for everyone who calls.

It is a job that you might get worse at, if you do too much of it. Clinicians who see patients all day every day cannot possibly do the listening work with the maximum possible engagement. For this reason I suspect most go though a reduction of intensity almost immediately in order to prevent a complete burnout, learning that they must stay protected and somewhat disengaged in order to keep going.

Agora

INCEPTION

Agora was founded in 1970 in response to a suicide on the University of New Mexico campus. In its first 52 years, about 5,000 volunteers have answered hundreds of thousands of calls, many of which were life changing moments for the people in crisis.

Barbara Blankenship, an Agoran in 1990, wrote about how it started:

> The impulse for a campus crisis center at the University of New Mexico was ignited by a student's suicide. The student had gone to the future founder of Agora, Dr. Frank Logan, who was the Chairman of the Psychology Department, with his fear that he was suicidal. Logan, not being a clinical psychologist, urged him to see a faculty member who was qualified to help. The student was afraid this would affect his grades and Logan assured him, as depart-

ment chair, that this would not happen. He also contacted the faculty member, who was a clinical psychologist, and told him if the student did not go to him, that he was to go to the student. The student went home and shot himself.

This was shocking. The student shared his fears. He received sound advice with committed follow-through. What went wrong? What was missing? Why did the student not get help from his professor? As a result of this suicide, Agora was begun. Logan and some faculty members realized they were "increasingly called on to provide emergency psychological aid to students and they felt that some psychological first aid and referral service should be available on a systematic basis."

The first faculty director was Dr. Samuel Roll, a psychologist with a strong Freudian leaning, and an intellectual multi-disciplinarian who brings philosophical history into daily practice. Ms. Blankenship quoted Dr. Roll's memory of the political climate in 1970:

When asked if he could paint a picture of campus life back in 1970 in relation to the inception of a crisis center, Dr. Roll responded that "there was a greater sense of excitement and vivacity. Everything was much alive. People were convinced that what they were doing would have some impact. They were also frightened; students had been killed at Kent State and there was absolute questioning of all authority ... The most excitement of course was when the National Guard invaded the campus. They stabbed some students. There was a big red cross

> right in front of Agora. They attacked and gassed
> Agora."

The Kent State incident involved the Ohio National Guard
killing four unarmed students during a peace rally in May
of 1970. The shootings triggered walk-outs at hundreds of
universities and high schools across the country, with
participation by millions of students. One of the first Agora
volunteers, David Dennedy-Frank, recalls that just before
Agora's inception, the university was shut down by protests
about Vietnam. A desire to do more constructive things
bloomed, as a way to work with the angst of the time. This
sense of possibility fueled new crisis centers across the
country at the time.

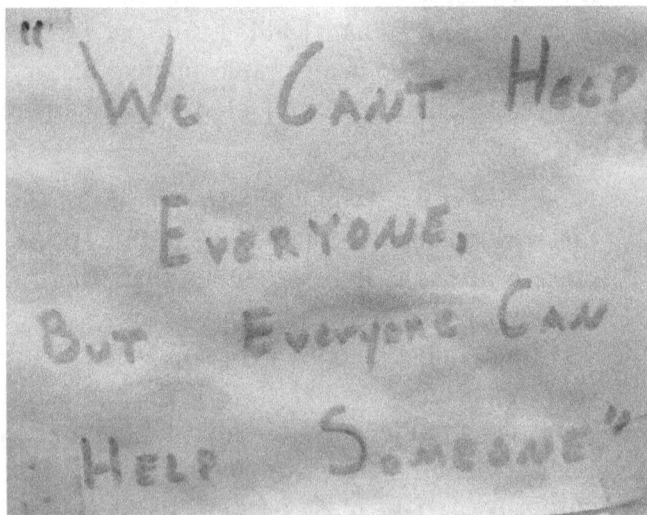

GROWTH AND CONTINUITY

Through the 70s and 80s, the faculty advisors were mostly short-term with nominal pay. A change occurred with the appointment of Dr. Martha Carmody, the clinical director who would serve 14 years starting in 1986. She helped with the organization's growth and continuity. She kept Agora extraordinarily focused on the simple truth that skillful active listening is a powerful and helpful tool to assist people in crisis. Agora kept this principle at the forefront and has remained a viable service ever since, while other university based crisis centers got pulled in different directions and did not fare as well.

Molly Brack started volunteering in 1991 and became friends with Martha, who identified her as a potential future leader. Martha told me, "I felt really good about leaving Agora with the idea of her taking over."

Molly took the director position in 2000, holding it for the next 22 years. As the first full-time director, she can be credited with substantial growth and securing more and larger funding sources.

MOLLY

When meeting the people at Agora, Molly reflected, "I found my tribe." There were only a half dozen volunteers, but in her tenure, the numbers rose to the hundreds, and now we even turn away volunteers regularly.

In 2001, after the 9/11 tragedy, the phones started ringing a lot. Molly called on past volunteers to come in. Call volume went from 10 to 100 calls per day. A training that only six students had signed up for ballooned to 45 on the first day of training. That momentum has stayed with Agora through the present day.

Molly is also a doula, which is the service of being present with someone in childbirth, one of the most painful and life-changing moments of their life. She is present in these moments as a person who listens, receives, and reflects, but does not direct.

Her belief in volunteerism comes from knowing how giving selflessly changes a person. It is not just because of a lack of money to pay people. Significant volunteering has been essential throughout her life and Agora is a way to bring that to others, many of whom have not grown up with a volunteering ethic in their families.

She told me that the two most touching things that she wants the world to know about Agora are the tightness of community among the Agorans, and the selfless dedication of so many of the volunteers to the mission.

Mia Mendoza, an Agoran who was trained in counseling and social work, and now is a force for change in mental health systems, attributes the magic of Molly to "her ability to connect to anyone, so that person feels seen and cared for. And she has trained others to do the same. She sees the potentials of everyone around her, nurtures their motivation, and always wants the best for them."

Agora office

EDGE OF VIABILITY

Agora has a habit of forever teetering on the edge of viability; funding sources come and go and it adjusts what it can do based on that. It has had to move a few times in its history as "more important things" needed the space.

In 2000, some leaders in the university made an effort to shut Agora down. Molly called around for a lifeline, and the psychology advisor, Dan Mathews, saved it by letting Agora move into a converted garage. That cozy, though marginal, space is where Agora still runs today.

In a letter to the Albuquerque Journal, the Agora Advisory Board wrote:

> Agora has time and again asked UNM to fund its operating budget of less than $ 65,500 per year to provide some stability to its operation. (This figure is less than 10% of outgoing coach Rocky Long's $671,000 severance expense.) The answer, as recently as last month, has been a resounding "NO." Why? Simple – Agora does not make money. Agora does not conduct research. Agora is not an academic enterprise. It merely provides a valuable service to the UNM community, Albuquerque, and outlying areas. That's all. Apparently, fulfilling UNM's mission of service to others doesn't warrant support from the University.

Strangely, while for-profit and other professional centers can secure millions annually in funding, the much more efficient model of Agora has trouble staying afloat. For the price of one single professional salary and one assistant, Agora can manage hundreds of volunteers to take thousands of calls. The cost comparison to for-profit centers is not even close.

Molly says "The thing that saves Agora every year is that it is magical." She has visited many dozens of crisis centers in the US and none are quite like us. "Something about Agora spirit draws in people who are looking for community and want to give their time to help strangers. People who join get in touch with their compassion and courage – this keeps us going."

Martha says there are two miracles: that lives are saved, and that an organization can squeak its way through every budget issue, and continue to be there for what it implored itself to do.

ENOUGH TIME

There have been other student-led crisis centers but none have lasted this long and no others are currently serving the general public. Volunteering in this capacity is on the decline, but Agora remains centered on volunteers, supported by paid staff.

The most striking difference between what Agora does and what many other centers do is that Agora allows time for the relationship and trust to build – time for a connection to be meaningful, equal, and respectful. Calls are often longer than a half hour, and occasionally even longer than two hours. Text based chats are frequently over an hour. It can take more than a few minutes to build rapport and feel that one is in a safe haven. This is enough time to actually rekindle hope or feel the power of healing. Only rarely is a crisis substantially resolved in one call, but it is important that a person has the time to sense an opening and find the direction they need for a next step.

Other centers, and especially those answering 988 calls, are well funded and efficient machines, meaning they resolve the call as quickly as possible by referrals to other professionals. While Agora calls have the openness of a lazy summer day without a deadline, some other centers are trying to keep their call times to 3-7 minutes, more like a hectic Burger King drive through. That is not a model of rekindling hope, and hardly even time to build rapport with a counselor.

Historically most people who called crisis lines never got through, because the number of volunteers has never been enough to meet the demand. That is one reason why efficiency may be appealing – at least each person in need gets to talk to someone for a few minutes. Thankfully with 988 funding, the queues are short and people are getting through. Some people get the referral they need, but I suspect most people leave in the same state of mind that they came with. Efficiency measured at the level of an individual interaction is not even meaningful. A single long call that uplifts someone so much that they no longer need to call in is time better spent than many calls from the same person who keeps trying because the roots of the crisis were never addressed.

While we can count and log calls with demographic categories and make spreadsheets with graphs, we cannot really measure the true results of those encounters with numbers. The efficient centers may try to measure success numerically and downplay what cannot be measured. Neither model gives us a way to graph the life force or know if the person who called really made a permanent course correction in life. We do not know if they took their life or not; when the call is over, we let go. But we still know that Agora is effective because a consistent stream of comments from callers tell us that Agora is the only place they get real help without judgment.

Mia says Agora "provides a space where the world can stop for a minute." This is critical when someone feels the walls closing in or feels urgently suicidal; it can feel like our interactions create time where there was none.

ANY TOPIC, NO SCREENING

In some 988 crisis centers, there is a focus on triage, or screening calls to find out if the crisis is acute, so they can efficiently end less necessary calls. For people in a suicide crisis, often the brain's center of reasoning is not working well, resulting in not being able to say quickly what the issue is or how acute it is. Being asked questions about how bad the problem is can feel extremely stressful and judgmental.

At Agora, callers can talk about anything and we do not steer or judge how important their issue is. A seemingly trivial topic to start with can be a way to get into the mental space where one is ready to go into deeper things. Many times callers have been unable to even say what is bringing them down, but after a while the dots start connecting. Sometimes they even start by saying they are fine, but they are not at all fine. If we cut people off because they are not acting like someone in a "real crisis" then we would never have the time to get to what the real crisis is.

Mia told me that Agora shines in addressing the more difficult topics, where even some masters level programs do not teach how to address them well. For example, we ask directly: "Are you thinking about suicide?" It turns out that asking someone who is thinking about it can be so welcome when someone has been pressured to keep it hidden. When someone is not thinking about it, they just say no; it does not "give them the idea" to take their life, so we do not need to avoid the topic.

Likewise with sexual assault, we listen to anything. We do not pry about details, or try to label something as "rape" or pressure any specific resolution. Instead we stay with their own telling of what happened with its confusion and complexity. While it is OK if they want to be specific about the perpetrator's acts, victims tend to be more focused on their feelings, attached meanings, and future safety.

PARAPROFESSIONAL VOLUNTEERS

Dasie Kent, the current associate director, pointed out that when she has called crisis lines in the past, it was a mixed bag. Some of the professionally-staffed lines would only talk if she explicitly said she was in crisis, and they gave quick referrals. "I feel that Agora is special in that we can talk to anyone at any level of crisis. I think many callers appreciate that we're there to listen and reflect so they are empowered to make their own decisions in their respective situations."

Agora's model is between the professional and the untrained peer model – we have enough solid training to be sure the listeners are good at listening, but still staffed by volunteers.

The term "paraprofessional" has been used historically to denote that middle level of training with supervision, thought it has fallen out of use.

Each student volunteer is drawn because of some story in their history, and they are looking for community and their own healing at a pivotal time in their life. Volunteers take the commitment very seriously, and do not want to let their fellow students down.

We do not pretend to be any more healthy than people who call in, and we can admit our own problems. When a lot of volunteers stay for a long time without being paid, that is a proof that we are getting something else from the experience.

DURABLE PHILOSOPHY

The training manual introduces Agora like this:

> Agora advocates unconditional acceptance for each individual. The minimal guarantee we make to our clients is that they will be accepted under every circumstance and without reservation. We are non-judgmental and do not try to impose our own personal values on anyone else. This does not mean you deny or give up any of your own beliefs and values, but rather you give others the opportunity to work on an issue without fear or judgment. When people feel that they can speak freely and without fear of judgment or criticism, they will be able to

put their problems out in the open and often get a new understanding of them. Your role at Agora is to be a good listener and provide others a non-threatening opportunity to express themselves and begin to work toward resolution on their own. When people feel free to be open and trusting, they develop the confidence to work things out with the counselor as a facilitator. This empowers them to have greater skills in solving problems on their own in the future and conveys to them that they are worthy and competent. Giving someone advice or telling him or her what to do in a situation is never helpful. We want to encourage our callers to use their own inner resources in dealing with life's difficulties.

Molly is not one to be swept up in the latest fad philosophy about anything. The consistency of Agora over decades is remarkable, and I believe the old-fashioned values are a key to understanding why it works so well. As I will discuss in later chapters, she has not adopted modern social justice language or ideology, or the pressures of professionalizing. While it remains pretty constant, it never gets into a rut.

The only thing she says that changed in philosophy over her tenure is becoming more conscious of boundaries, which includes limits on abusive or sexual language.

Molly says: "I'm attached to the original idea of time to connect to another human for as long as they need." She is not prone to even attempting to articulate abstract philosophy, which may be why this book needed to be written by someone else. She downplays herself as the moral compass of the organization, though everyone else understands that she is. She does not claim any allegiance to a popular theory; she just believes in being with people in life's most precious and terrible moments – the highs and the lows – even if the person is unintelligible, angry, or silent. She would sit with someone who is dying with no appeal to efficiency or theory, just because they are a human who deserves to die with the dignity of companionship. "No one should have to die alone" – this statement may be the most concise way to express what her philosophy is.

The fact that Agora principles have not changed in generations speaks to how inspired the founders were – Dr. Logan, Dr. Roll, and others.

CO-LEADING

When I ask about all the other people who have contributed to Agora over the years, Molly immediately comes up with many names, and talks about their unique perspectives, their energy and dedication, their humor and light. She is apparently in competition with no one, and can flex to work with nearly any personality.

I suspect she downplays or does not see her own influence on all these people – how her love and appreciation infects them and allows them to bring their perspectives, energy, and light.

The first associate director, Jeremy, was a co-lead with Molly when she first started. Jeremy was an undergraduate who led another student organization promoting contraceptives and sexual health, which clashed with the abstinence-only policy of the administration at the time. Agora had been small, and Jeremy was well connected and was the key person who increased Agora's training program to hundreds of students per semester. To me it is remarkable that a director on university staff could so effectively work with an undergraduate as equals, and give him space to do what he could do best. This early example of appreciating someone enough to unlock their ability to contribute great things has been repeated many times over since then.

For me personally, she is the most special mentor I have had. I have lasted with Agora much longer than I have normally lasted with any organization, and I have become a more compassionate person. Her leadership model, which I will spell out more in a later chapter, is a blueprint for many kinds of organizations. She is a true servant leader and educator in the best way. The model of learning by doing in a student club has, for me, been a more valuable kind of education than any college class.

RADICAL

Unassuming old-fashioned values usually do not get labeled as "radical," but what really is radical?

A servant leader does not look like a leader; they may seem like an assistant, maybe even overlooked. A radical experiment can appear mainstream. The true function and outcome of something can be obscured by the absence of a glossy exterior. By the same token, so-called radical progressive activism can sometimes be composed mainly of a glossy exterior whose actual function perpetuates the same system that it claims to fight. We have to look far below the surface of things to discover if they are radical, disruptive, or threatening to the social order.

I felt drawn to Agora because of its radical position in this world, even though it is packaged in an aging, unmarked, undersized, shed-like building. We are "just" listening to people, but it is the focus on that, along with all the things we are *not* doing, that makes it radical. We are not judging; we are not sidetracked into excessive numerical measurements; we are not fixing; and we are not drawing attention to how radical this is.

EMERGENCY-NON-EMERGENCY GAP

Agora helps fill the gap between non-emergency and emergency level support. The system of help in the US is full of gaps; it is more accurate to say that there is a collection of disparate kinds of help, but they do not comprise an actual *system*. As a result of deinstitutionalization in the 1980s, New Mexico has no true coordinated system of care, and there are not enough spaces in lower-intensity residential treatment centers. Thus people are being served in higher-intensity hospitals, or find their way out of state, or end up in prisons, or forego care.

The same is true of healthcare in general: The US lacks a coordinated healthcare system. It can feel like there are so many gaps that it becomes a canyon landscape that is impossible to traverse. When we give referrals on the phone, we cannot have confidence that when they call the various numbers we give out, that they will actually get the help they need.

One of the biggest and largely unrecognized gaps in the US system of help is the mismatch between the complexity of accessing the system and the state of mind of people needing to access it. When you are in a panic and do not know what you need, that is a time when it is impossible to navigate the maze of options, try to find a therapist, and so on. Crisis lines help fill that gap.

In a related way, the system of financial supports for disability is based on the cruel irony that those who are not able to file all the paperwork (possibly due to their disability) cannot get help through that system. You must prove that you are not capable of holding a job by going through complex bureaucratic processes, which, if you could achieve, would be evidence of being capable of holding a job. Consequently many people require lawyers to get assistance at all. The gaps in income support and many other types of social services cannot be filled by a crisis line, but the idea of services filling those gaps can extend to all these other areas.

TEXT OR CALL

People can choose voice calls or text for crisis help. The 988 number accepts both. As one would expect, younger people choose texting far more than older. The average age on text is about 16 while the average on voice is closer to 30.

When I starting text-based counseling I was afraid that it would feel distant – not being able to hear and use tone of voice could restrict the connection. But that turned out to be unfounded because there are other things you can do with typing that you cannot do with voice. Mainly, you can delay (you do not need to worry about the cadence of a conversation), collect your thoughts, and choose what to reveal. People using text actually tend to reveal a lot more a lot quicker than on voice. I imagine that a texter might be locked in her bedroom, feeling like she is in a void away from the world and people, where she can choose when and how much to say, and she has more control over the communication link. This might allow her to stay in her own mindspace much more easily. On the phone, it feels more like being in public, so you can lose that very personal mindspace and be self-conscious of how you are sounding.

In any effective crisis conversation, whether voice or text, the center of it has to stay with the caller. An analogy for that is the idea of the center of gravity of a system of two asteroids: If they are equal size, the center of gravity is in the middle, but if one is larger, the center is closer to the larger asteroid. If a counselor is demanding information or pushing advice, it makes them larger and pulls the center of gravity away. Voice calls risk that, especially if the protocol requires getting demographic information at the beginning. Texting can minimize that risk and make sure the counselor is in orbit around the caller, and not the other way around.

APPRECIATIONS

People of all stripes have expressed what Agora has done for them. Here is a tiny sample of what we have heard.

Some are notes from volunteers, and some are directly from callers:

- Caller was very grateful to have someone to talk to that didn't think she was a weirdo. Said she was feeling better at the end of the call.

- He really, really appreciated that I was not there to judge him ... He was so grateful just to be able to talk it out with someone and was very kind to me. He left me with a giant grin on my face.

- He said it's helpful for him to call Agora to have his feelings validated, and getting that done keeps him from getting suicidal.

- He was very appreciative of Agora volunteers. Said being able to just talk without any judgment is a wonderful thing for him.

- I am so glad this line exists. I used to call an ambulance every time I had a panic attack and they would tell me I was fine. Talking on this line really helps calm me down.

- I don't know if I would've made it without you all at Agora. Everyone is so kind, but I've never met anyone like you, you are so smart.

- I feel understood, it is a great relief. You've put humpty-dumpty back together again.

- I really respect what you're doing, I mean I really commend you for taking the time to listen to other people's problems when you have to go home and deal with your own problems too. Really, that's cool as shit. It has been really helpful talking with you.

- When her son drowned, a night shift Agoran is what saved her. She likes Agora because she does not feel threatened about disclosing her identity.

- Says we have fairy dust that makes things better.

- She said that Agora has gotten her through the last six months with the will to live.

- She said that knowing that someone is out there to reassure her that she is not crazy and that her feelings are understandable and that she is entitled to them was the best thing that she could have heard. She seemed very grateful to have found out about the magic of the Agora Crisis Center.

- She thanked me for being there and letting her have someone to talk to. She made a comment about the fact that we are the only warm line in the country that is willing to talk to people like her. She's grateful for that.

- The caller was very thankful; we went from extreme panic to laughing at the end of the call. She had called four other suicide hotlines before calling Agora and was put on hold. She was thankful for the talk and decompression this morning and now has our number saved and will be calling in the future.

- This line has been tremendous to me, I can't imagine being alive without it. She did a really wonderful job and I didn't think she could do it, but she brought me up from being so low.

- You saved my life tonight.

MAKE CONTACT

If you would like to make contact with Agora, you can call 505-277-3013 or find us on-line at www.agoracares.org.

Trauma

CRISIS

The Agora training manual defines a crisis thus:

> People give meaning to the events that happen in
> their lives. Each of us witnessing or participating in
> the same event will experience it differently. When
> we attempt to help someone in crisis, it is important
> to try to understand the event from their perspec-
> tive, not how we would feel if it were happening to
> us. Any life event can take on crisis proportions if it
> is experienced as sudden, intense, unexpected or
> emotionally super-charged. We experience crisis as
> overwhelming, leaving us without means to cope or
> to adjust. Somehow, we cannot make sense of what
> is happening or why it is happening. Without
> answers to those important questions, we are left
> helpless. We simply do not know what to do to
> control or master the situation. We do not know

how to make it stop. Wave after wave of emotion sweeps over us and we are unable to predict when or if this awful situation is going to end. Thus, any event can be a crisis if it wipes out our ability to make sense of what is happening. We feel helpless, and unable to gain mastery over our lives. It is only after we regain some sense of understanding and some sense of control that the crisis can be reduced to something manageable.

Importantly, crisis is not something that can be avoided or that we should try to eliminate. It is part of the mechanics of human growth to reach a sticking point and then find a deep course correction. What we can and should do, however, is help people move through a crisis and rise from it: every crisis is a growth opportunity. Whenever I imply that crisis is a bad thing, it is shorthand for saying that being stuck for a long time in crisis in a bad thing.

TRAUMA AND MEMORY

People in extreme crisis are not having a bad day or a bad week; they are having a bad life. By a "bad life" I mean one that has not prepared them for a successful bad day.

A toddler who falls might look up to his mother to see how bad it is, before reacting. If she reacts strongly, he may burst out in tears, perhaps feeling responsible for making her feel bad. But if she takes it in stride with an "oopsie daisy" – allowing him to express his hurt – then he may move beyond it more quickly. This tells us that pain, even physical pain, is social: the experience of processing hurt is a lot about communication, both receptive and expressive.

With an ideally healthy psyche, we have a life sprinkled with bad days, and we express the pain as we go along. Even as we grow up and the bad things get bigger and bigger, we can remain resilient. We might cry or yell or find other ways to communicate feelings; importantly all that expression has to be near the time of the negative experience, since it is an exercise of cleaning or maintaining psychological health.

Anything that interrupts this well-maintained system causes an accumulation of unexpressed emotions, and this leads to psychic complexity and reduced resilience. All the unfinished business is poised to turn the next bad thing into a crisis. The difference between psychic trauma and all other hurts is not defined by the intensity; it is defined by the process of recovery in the aftermath. When we express and resolve quickly (even if the thing that happened is huge) then it is not a trauma, but when we suppress the aftermath with too little resolution, it becomes trauma. If the toddler fell over and the mother prevents any expression about it with "don't cry" or a tacit threat, the healing does not happen. It is vital for him to express whatever he is feeling without being prompted about the "right" way to feel.

One way to distinguish trauma from other bad memories is the way it is remembered, or not remembered. Traumatic memories come with a surge of emotion, or a sensation of re-experiencing the past hurt. They are painful to remember and retell. Other memories of bad experiences do not have that intense emotional grip. The trauma memories may be conscious, partly conscious, or repressed. When traumatic memory is repressed, it is still there, waiting to be brought to consciousness, and still acting in your psyche.

The term "trigger" is possibly overused today to mean anything that is offensive or uncomfortable, but its root meaning is a current action or exposure that activates a repressed memory and brings it closer to consciousness. A trigger is generally unwanted because it brings up painful memories, but on the other hand it can be useful as a way to find out what memories are repressed.

In addition to the phenomenon of the emotion surge, traumatic memories can be split in such a way that the factual account is remembered but the feelings are repressed. Someone might flatly say, "I was locked in a basement for years," but also not really have anything to share about it, as if it had happened to someone else. While part of the facts have been remembered, the full story and feelings are still buried and the healing has not started.

HOW WE GET TRAUMATIZED

To generalize, trauma happens due to a failure to express and process emotions at the time they first arise. What follows talks about some forces that pressure us to defer and not express.

One reason is systemic oppression built into society. One of the mechanisms of oppression in a society beset with inequity is to socially erase knowledge about trauma. I heard a theory from a student of history that over the course of generations and empires, there has been a constant rediscovery of trauma and all the language of healing. According to this theory, within each cycle, it gets rediscovered and named, becomes popular and better understood (as is happening now), but then it becomes threatening to the elite and gets purged. If all the governments and social systems were operating with knowledge of trauma, we would inevitably address the systematic roots, leading to greater equality. Equality is a threat to the elite; a substantial part of politics is the elite class instilling fear in others using spurious threats to prevent equality. We can see today that there are explicit laws being passed to prevent teaching children about the ultimate inequality of slavery. Officials prevent this teaching by mischaracterizing grade school lessons as "Critical Race Theory" (CRT), then misunderstanding CRT to be an anti-white propaganda tool, then banning it on the basis of its alleged reverse racism. This series of fear-based fallacies, regardless of its conscious intent, has the effect of cracking down on self-knowledge about trauma and healing.

The message of oppression is: "You are suffering because of something inherently and permanently wrong with you, not because of anything done to you, so do not try to name the oppressor or heal from it."

That messaging can be replicated on an individual scale; for example, a man is using such gaslighting language to a woman to keep her confused, self-doubting, and obedient. It involves the same crackdown against healing and plays out in a relationship that she is trapped in. The individual and society-wide versions of this work in essentially the same way at different scales.

A connected dynamic that drives deferral and prevents healing is taboos. Briefly a taboo is a form of society-level repression of a subject, which we have a consensus agreement not to talk about. If you are not allowed to talk about something connected to your own trauma, you really cannot do the expression part of the healing. To understand this through an example, consider the two crimes: rape and arson. Sentencing for these may not be so different, and as such we can conclude that society has classified these at similar levels of badness. Nevertheless, people feel completely different about the two crimes and talk about them differently. People can talk about arson unemotionally and discuss motives, what to do about it, and so on. But with rape, especially if it is a child victim, people are so consumed by the taboo that the revulsion can overpower the ability to talk about it rationally.

Now summarizing some of the forces that pressure us to defer healing instead of expressing pain:

- Isolation

- Minority status: Being a member of a minority group is possibly in itself a reason why we live in continuous trauma, although maybe not all minorities do. It could come from being consistently devalued or marginalized, hiding, thinking of ourselves as not normal.

- Disability: Disabled people are sometimes co-labeled with PTSD (post-traumatic stress disorder), and it could be misleading to suggest that the PTSD is something separate from the disability. Being disabled is being powerless, and that is in itself what is continuously traumatic.

- Objectification: Growing up thinking about ourselves too much as objects (how we appear and whether we fulfill the needs of others), rather than subjects (what we want for ourselves), can lead us to be so out of balance that it becomes a powerless state, and is continuous trauma. ("Who am I if he doesn't love me?")

- Parenting: Being repeatedly told not to express bad things, or being punished for doing so, drives those things underground.

- Danger: Physical danger (living in a war zone or near/ with people who are violent) that one cannot get out of keeps someone from expressing the feelings about it.

INTERSECTIONAL TRAUMA

Incest, which is rape from family members, is considered worse than other rape because the people you might go to for help are the very people hurting you. This blocks the possibility of healing through expression to parents. It is worse because the parenting is traumatizing on top of the original victimization. A child might only have school as a model of positive living if every other way they turn is dangerous.

But consider if abuse is happening at school as well; such a child could feel that the entire world is dangerous and the trauma gets sealed in much deeper.

It can get even worse: religious or ritual abuse shuts off any recourse from a higher power by teaching the victim that they are an incarnation of irredeemable sin. People usually want to escalate a problem upstairs somehow: children tell an older sibling, teacher, or parent about a problem. Failing that, they can go to the principal or grandparent. Adults can go to the boss, the boss's boss, the courts, the priest... there is always a higher level to seek a solution from. But when all those levels are complicit in victimizing you, then there is no one to go to.

I have a friend who was trafficked, and could not go to the police because she was being raped by them; she could not go to the church because she was being raped by them, too.

Under those conditions, a person splits into many people, each with fragmented memories. It is impossible to repress everything and have no consciousness at all, while remaining alive. One of the final strategies we have to live with trauma when all routes to expression are blocked is to divide consciousness itself.

Suicide

UNITED STATES IS AN OUTLIER

The suicide rate in the US has gone up over the last 20 years while it has gone down most everywhere else.

South Korea, Lithuania, Russia, and Guyana are some of the few countries that have had much higher rates than the world trend. I included South Korea on the chart as an example of the large variance between countries. Most other countries have experienced a decrease in suicide for a few decades.

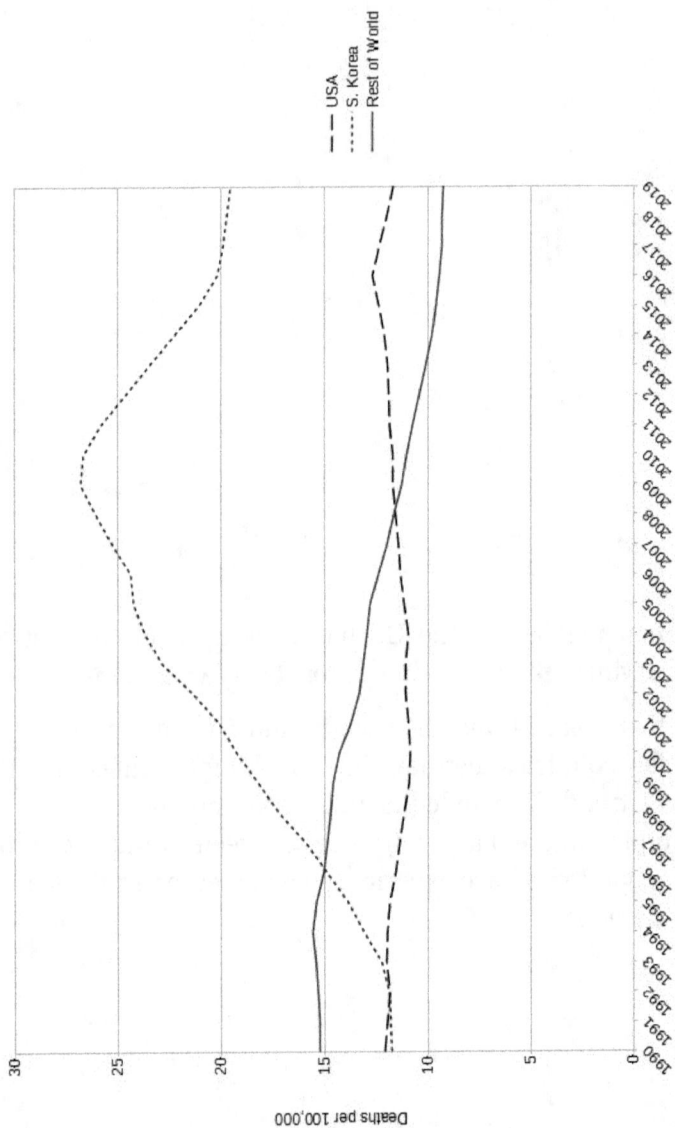

You may have heard alarming statistics – for example, that the US suicide rate has gone up about 30% in the 20 years before 2017. This is true, but looking at the graph, we can see that the statistic was hand-picked to highlight the years with the most change. In order not to be alarmist, I included data before that and put it in perspective in the graph. This highlights a conclusion that is more important than the 30% statistic: that the US has not achieved the reduction that most of the rest of the world has achieved.

The failure exposed by these data suggests that the US has not really had much of a national response at all, or that a misunderstanding of suicide crisis has led the US to take ineffective actions in response. People have blamed narrow factors like social media, and while that may contribute to depression, it does not answer why the US is so different: social media is everywhere.

This book does not attempt to give a single answer that explains why, but it does include some perspectives on the health system, and extreme social justice culture, which could be linked to the reason. The US is distinctive in that we have no real national health care system – we just have a patchwork of laws and programs that do not compose a coordinated whole. We do not give any single democratic body the responsibility to respond to national health problems. Related to that, the US culture is individualistic in a way that makes cooperative community management difficult across all areas of public life. Political polarization has also been more extreme in the US in recent years than in other countries,[1] and other research has come out linking

---

1   Boxell, Levi & Gentzkow, Matthew & Shapiro, Jesse M. Cross-Country Trends in Affective Polarization. National Bureau of Economic Research 2020.

political polarization to mental health. Because of the polarization, Americans are more likely to spread misinformation on social media, perhaps exacerbating the negative effects of social media here.

In the graph above, data are not "age adjusted." Different countries have different ratios of young, middle, and older people, and in order to compare different populations accurately, statisticians adjust numbers slightly to account for those ratios. An age-adjusted graph would look only slightly different.

Related to our piecemeal healthcare system, some suggest that the higher US suicide rate could be related to for-profit corporate structures. With her experience in a variety of clinical structures, Dr. Martha Carmody names the profit motive as a big factor in allowing people to slip through the cracks: corporate medicine inevitably sets up barriers to service, with payment guarantees being a primary one. Patient identification, insurance information and diagnosis all has to be secured, which delays a compassionate response to those in critical need of assistance.

THE STATISTICS

For those who like statistics, you can find data and sources at the American Psychological Association – www.apa.org – or the National Institute of Mental Health – www.nimh.nih.gov. The items that stand out to me as the most important to know are:

- The US response has not been effective in the last two decades, as noted above.

- Middle-aged white men are the largest single demographic category of suicides. Notably this is also the demographic that owns the most guns, and firearms are used in about half of suicides. This suggests that availability of guns in the US (which is far higher than in most places) is a contributing factor.

- Suicide is the second leading cause of death in teens and young adults – meaning it is a national crisis, not something we can ignore or should expect.

- States with the highest rates include all the mountain states (including New Mexico, where Agora is located) and West Virginia. This suggests that one risk factor may be the combination of poverty and low density.

WHY SUICIDE

People do not take their own life because of a single bad thing that happened, or even many bad things. It cannot be blamed solely on depression, or any mental health condition, or on poverty. It can be confusing to understand why some people do it; some wealthy people whose situations look perfect from the outside take their lives even though they appear to have everything going for them – a family, education, and opportunities. At the same time, other people who are repeatedly victimized and have next to nothing might have no thoughts of suicide.

The most common factors in people who think about suicide are trauma, isolation, loss, and lack of autonomy. If I had to pick one single explanation, it would be having one's autonomy so restricted that steering one's own life has become impossible. I will get into this in more detail later in the book, but for now the main point is that suicide always remains an option when there are no options. If terrible things happen, but you can react and make changes ("steer"), then you have options.

Consider this choice: Would you rather be locked inside a fancy estate for the rest of your life with an unlimited buffet and every other amenity, or be free but penniless? For many people, freedom is worth more than everything else.

The lack of options can happen in any social class. It can be due to an overly controlling partner or family, which is an imprisonment of the body. It can also be an imprisonment in the mind, based on trauma causing the belief that one has no options.

Death by suicide has to be understood in its larger context of death by despair, which also includes accidental drug overdoses and reckless behavior. Those deaths, even if labeled accidental, also occur because of having the sense of no other options, leading people to treat their own life as unworthy of protection. Whether it is an intentional suicide or an accident in a state of despair is not the most important distinction.

Stephanie Ramsey, a long-time Agoran who now teaches college, calls the problem of finding the reasons for changes in suicide rates "a chaotic problem," meaning it is multi-variable and so complex that it is not possible to untangle or reduce to simple numbers or reasons.

Mia Mendoza, being another systems thinker in this arena, points out some of the factors where the US differs from other wealthy countries: more people in poverty, social polarization, rampant targeting of minorities, threats and violence everywhere, and a general collapse of institutions of health and education. We live in a more traumatic environment in the US where more people are losing hope and cannot see a better future.

Categories

This chapter looks at patterns of age and gender and how they relate to personal crisis.

GENDER

Patterns of despair are quite different for males and females. Inmates in prisons are over 99% male, while mental hospitals house about even numbers of males and females. The rate of mental illness diagnosed in women is somewhat higher, and women access both physical and mental health services more often than men. At the same time, around 70% of suicides are male.

To a counselor, suicide looks like a predominantly female *problem*, but it is more accurate to say that counseling is a female-oriented *solution*. Girls and women call into Agora somewhat more, comprising about 60% of phone calls, while about 80% of teens accessing help by text are female. We are able to help most people who call (or text) to some degree, and it appears that females are getting this help more effectively, while males are less likely to reach out, and are more likely to feel they have nowhere to go for the kind of help they need.

These differences make sense when we think about some of the basic gender patterns – at least as they are expressed in the US. Males have more rage and tend to take action more impulsively, and tend to emphasize personal space and power over others. Women tend to be be more relational, defining themselves through connections to others. Men are far more likely to divert internal problems into physical control of others, or violence against others, and also to take their own lives. With teens, girls are more likely to cut themselves (or other forms of harm) and use physical pain as a relief from psychological pain. As a very broad general-ization, women are more likely to blame themselves, take responsibility for themselves and others, try to solve prob-lems with repeated attempts over a longer period of time, and delay suicide.

Possibly the biggest single difference is women's much higher tendency to reach out and talk, trust a counselor, and be open to the power of that kind of relationship. It is easy to say, "if only men would open up, they could get help too" – but a lot of men are not like that and will not conform to a system that has been built to help women. Men take longer to reveal personal things, and may blame counselors more, and occasionally get aggressive towards us as counselors. While we can help men a lot of the time, the fact that 70% of suicides are male reveals a giant gap in the system: we are not as good at helping people who have issues with rage and aggression.

"The loneliest people are the kindest. The saddest people smile the brightest. The most damaged people are the wisest. All because they do not wish to see anyone else suffer the way they do."

Unknown

American men's enrollment in college is declining compared with women's, they are getting worse grades, and gradually losing their traditional hold on higher-level jobs. In conservative "men's rights" circles, there are endless complaints that schools and workplaces are becoming feminized and that this is resulting in men losing their "place in society." For those of us who favor equality, it is easy to mock or dismiss their loss of privilege, but there is still a truth there that needs attention. Without a shared cultural concept of masculinity that boys can grow up into and feel empowered and wanted, we are at risk of breeding a generation of disconnected and dangerous people.

I was once in a group of women in an office, and over a partition wall we could hear two men speaking in very masculine language – lots of "brother" and "man up" and daring to take the bull by the horns. A laugh ricocheted through our side of the partition, acknowledging (1) that it was funny how different it sounded from how we would talk, (2) that one of them was supporting the other effectively, and (3) that the women could not do what they were doing the same way.

At the end of the book I will include some thoughts about how to better serve men in crisis.

NONTRADITIONAL GENDERS

In 2021 a leap occurred in the number of teens who identify themselves as transgender or non-binary. Based on my own call history, it jumped from 1% to around 20%. Before that year, most people who identified that way also talked about their gender as the primary problem they were experiencing. Since that time, a whole new and larger set of people identify as a nontraditional gender but do not experience it as a problem.

I personally doubt that the deeply male and female patterns of being have changed in our culture in such a short time; rather, the words have changed meanings. A generation ago, hardly anyone said they were non-binary, even though many people have always had characteristics of both genders. Now many more people are using that word, but the distribution of people over the spectrum of gender has likely remained more constant.

Most people talk in a distinctly female or male way, and we usually have a very clear feeling that we are talking to a male or female. Even over text when they have not mentioned their gender, it often becomes obvious fairly quickly. Sometimes the gender patterns never show up because some few people really are truly non-binary – not on one side or the other – and we have to avoid the urge to pigeonhole them.

What if someone identifies themselves as a trans-boy but it feels completely like talking to a girl – or vice versa? In progressive circles, it might be said that it is imperative to speak to a trans-boy like any other boy, or in general affirm however people identify themselves. But I have to push back on that, and this point goes way beyond gender: We need to avoid being sidetracked by gender labels (or any category) and connect in the most genuine way we can to the whole human without assumptions. As an example that illustrates the complexity of gender, a trans-boy might have the experience of being sexually targeted because people see him as a girl. We deal with that *experience*, without dwelling on the labels.

AGE PATTERNS

Age plays a big role in the type of crisis and how we connect to callers. Up until age 20 to 25, most people have the experience of reaching milestones of learning, and of creating or discovering things about themselves exactly once. In other words everything is always new, life is linear, and each thing builds on the last thing. After that age, people start going in cycles, going back to the same feelings and problems that they may have already been through or solved before. It stops being linear and there are multiple experiences one can look back on to compare. What this means for younger people in their linear phase is that a single experience is interpreted as all experiences – for example, if one person loves me then everyone loves me, or if one person breaks up with me, then that loss is my entire life and is permanent. A pre-teen in suicide crisis looks very different than others, because their issue seems small (if we are a lot older), but to them it is a life-or-death-sized issue. For example, the first time a friend causes a rift in the friend group, or a relative dies, that fact is the apex of their linear life to date; therefore it seems like the only thing that is true at that time. An eleven-year-old could easily contemplate suicide just because two best friends became better friends with each other and failed to invite her somewhere after school. As counselors we need to listen just the same and treat them the same as an adult, because the caller is always in charge of what is important to them. We do not judge the size of their issue or try to offer perspective compared to other people.

We do not offer more direction or guidance when the person in crisis is young. At the same time, we need to keep in mind that a loss of a friend or other "small" thing is not the actual root reason for thinking about suicide; the real reasons are always life-long and deeper, while the "small" (actually big) thing is the trigger. For example, if a friend problem triggers suicide thoughts, that could indicate emotional neglect from the mother, which gets closer to the root of it.

For mid-teens, the first loss of love is huge for many people, and is similar to the pre-teen example above. Teens frequently present as if they have emotionally distanced from parents, but usually parent relationships are still far more consequential than all others – the internalized voice of the parent is powerful. Parents often see their children as 2-3 years younger than the youth see themselves, so the difference in autonomy that is desired versus what is allowed is a huge and common trigger of a crisis.

One of the common issues in the age range of 17-24 or so (which is also an opportunity) is the issue of holding on to the childhood self concept, as enforced by parental relationships (which lag by a few years), and thus being held back – a form of loss of autonomy. That knot can be loosened by letting go of a past self and emerging as if from a cocoon as a new self, or a leveled-up version 2.0. This is the first nonlinear event in growing up; it is not quite a cycle but it is a jump up from a plateau, or the first disconnect from the previously neatly ordered linear progression of growing up. The crisis of feeling stuck and the opportunity of reemerging are psychically one and the same.

Adults over 30-35 usually have experience changing jobs, associations, relationships, and living situations a few times, and each of these opens up a new side of oneself. The reasons for making those changes might not be just practical, such as a change to earn more money, but because the old patterns were not effective in cracking the nut at the center of the previous stage of existence. People can gradually become aware of some festering problem hidden under an otherwise stable life, and they may get the "seven year itch" or a need to disrupt and retrench in order to crack that nut and get to a new level. Retrenchment is a healthy way to change and continue development in adulthood, but each time it involves giving up the certainty of the previous stage and embarking into the unknown.

In the 20s and 30s, there is often a crisis of the first retrenchment, when one is not yet accustomed to cycles of the psyche and there is not the confidence needed to embark on a change.

Older adults have the unavoidable predicament that almost all counselors are a lot younger than they are, so it is only possible for us to listen, but we often cannot feel their pains with the benefit of our own experience. In my 50s I am seeing glimpses of how older people see many sides of things. Earlier, I wondered why old people never seem to have any strong convictions, until I became aware that the convictions of youth are a side effect of only having ever seen one side of something. Older people are slower to act partly because they are weighing more perspectives.

I think every age group has secrets that are hidden from the younger groups, as if it is a conspiracy. An older sister may find joy in keeping the secret of Santa Claus away from a younger sibling, and most of us are guilty of that conspiracy. But in our collective defense, a very young child cannot grasp all the distinctions between truth, fantasy, and deceit, so it is not possible for us to come clean and really explain it. Likewise middle aged people know things that we cannot explain to idealistic 20s people, and the elderly cannot explain all the other dimensions that someone in my age category cannot yet see.

The suicide crisis of an older adult is often very different than what we are used to as counselors. Not many of them call us, though suicide happens at that age too. My mother-in-law suffered for years with physical illness, and then without notice, took her life to end that suffering. An older person's maturity means they will not be impulsive, and will more likely plan to carry it out effectively, as she did. Often the decision for suicide is because of illness or some situation that is known to be unfixable.

Another pattern also exists with older people – being stuck in crisis for years at a time with no change. The person is threatening to take their life any minute now, but after years the threat is no longer believable. It is as if the capacity to endure pain has become *too* developed, so they cannot or will not make any changes. One of the ways we estimate risk is remembering that past behavior is the best predictor of future behavior; living 60 years without attempting suicide makes the current crisis relatively lower risk, but the person is still in crisis, unable to effect a retrenchment.

We do not need to understand developmental psychology to help people in each age category, because being a listener does not depend on being an expert. However, understanding the kinds of crisis in different life stages can give us the calm resolve that each passage can be navigated, and our confident state of mind can transfer to the person who is closed in and only seeing the immediate problem. They need someone to hold their hand as they psychically go through tunnels and mountains; the hand-holder's sure knowledge that these journeys will open up into new lands is priceless.

CULTURE OF AGE

Being a counselor with someone in each of these developmental categories involves the same compassion. Since the basic emotions are innate and do not age, the young and old experience the same range of emotion, and experience loss and loneliness the same way. Vocabulary can differ a little, but not by much. I tend to speak to all callers as myself and do not excessively simplify anything based on age. It was surprising to me after the first few times talking to 11 and 12 year-olds that I noticed in retrospect that I was speaking in adult ways, and they were too. Even if I have lived four of their lifetimes, I do not have any more experience *feeling* things. The gap in vocabulary has shrunk in the last generation, as more information about mental health is available, and vocabulary around feelings and trauma has become more widespread.

Discrimination based on race and gender has gradually gained recognition as a problem, but not all -isms are equally recognized. Ageism (along with ableism) is still very much part of the culture in the sense that the experiences and teachings of children are routinely minimized. We conflate protection of children with belittling, when we should consider them as spiritual and emotional equals or even teachers. Or, put another way, we are not a culture that honors the wholeness of children.

Changes in parenting in the last generation have given youth more supervision, and likewise schools are becoming more secure in the military sense. Stephanie (the Agoran mentioned in the previous chapter) has been teaching long enough to see an annual increase in parents' emotional investment in grades, and says "everything is higher stakes now." Parents are increasingly involved in the management of the minutiae of their children's lives.

Many generations ago, there was not adolescence as it exists today; people were married and working much younger, with more freedom and more responsibility. Today's teens long to have more freedom from supervision, and this question is an ongoing conflict in families, though it cannot be balanced in isolation. Teens also long to be relevant – to contribute and have the contributions recognized. Finding the balance of freedom can be easier if we look for the balance of responsibility at the same time.

Actual dangers have not changed nearly as much as the culture around perceived danger has changed. At the extreme, a political talking point these days is how hundreds of thousands of children go missing every year. Some actually believe that the Democrats are eating all those children, but the reality is that only a few dozen are killed by their kidnappers, and the rest are located.

All these cultural factors underpin the kind of crisis I am seeing in youth – an unmet need for connection and relevance.

ETHNICITY

Ethnicity is not as big a factor in crisis as I originally thought it might be. It most often comes up when there is a clash of cultures or racism within a family. An example is one side of the family looking down on another side.

Even when it does not come up, it could be helpful for listeners to keep in mind that non-white callers will assume that the listener is most likely white, and might not trust the system to treat everyone equally. Also minorities can experience a collective trauma from systemic racism, but in my experience this is a minor factor in the source of a personal crisis.

Healing

HOW HEALING FROM TRAUMA WORKS

I have a friend who was repeatedly raped by her father around age 12, then repressed the memory for over ten years. During that time she made remarks to me about having "never seen an aroused man" and claiming to know very little about sex. She appeared to have no sex drive and no attractions, and others were not attracted to her; her sexuality was basically switched off. Freud explained this effect as a protection of the repression. In order to keep the terror from being re-experienced, not only does the rape itself have to be kept hidden from consciousness, but anything surrounding it has to be kept hidden too; thus the original pain is encapsulated in many layers of protection.

One day as an adult she remembered part of what her father did. As she was ready, more memories came until she remembered it all. This was a remarkable story for me to hear, because the repression was so complete, but then over some years working with a therapist, the healing process was also unusually complete. After that work she could talk about it openly, and her sexuality came to life. When she was a teenager, she had not yet felt what happened to her, so that pain was there waiting to be experienced; it can be deferred but cannot be avoided. She had to bring it back and re-experience it in order to feel it and heal from it. Because pain is social, she had to tell someone and be heard deeply in order for that healing to happen.

I tell people that healing from trauma is possible, when they think it cannot be done. I tell them it is necessary when they think they can defer it forever. And I tell them it takes work, but I can never give instructions for that work. People want to know "how can I heal?" – but it is so uniquely personal that no one else can lead the process.

I said that people in crisis are not having a bad day, but more accurately, they *are* having a bad day, and the source of the trouble is never from today, but is almost always connected to some un-healed trauma. If today is a little bit lousy, then maybe a pizza or some diversion will help. If it is really bad, maybe more rigorous coping skills come in handy. But if it is bad down to the core, bringing up thoughts of suicide, then no coping mechanisms and nothing in the current day can help; the old stuff has to be addressed. In suicide crisis work, it is possible to do what feels like a year of therapy in an hour, because being on the brink of death makes someone ready to remember, and to stop deferring. They can suddenly see connections between the old and the new, and life becomes a linear story line in which childhood inevitably channels a person into the present day for known, explainable reasons. Without that light switching on, it can feel like a series of separate instances of bad luck, and there is no rhyme or reason to why that person should be a target for so much victimization.

Another friend had a bicycle accident with a minor musculoskeletal injury in her leg. Life went on but the pain would come back sometimes. With massage it would come back a lot, but eventually with enough massage it was healed. This is an illustration that the same effect of repressed memory happens in the whole body, not just in what is normally considered the mind. The pain from the accident was for some reason not fully experienced at the time, so it was still there waiting to be experienced later. It was deferred but could not be avoided. It was healed only after it was felt in its entirety, and only in communication with another person. Massage (when done well) is a form of listening; the helper is asking the body what it needs and giving it time to express and heal itself. Massage, like talk therapy, should never be done to someone as a series of rehearsed steps; that would be like a therapist giving advice without listening to the problems the client expresses.

RETELLING

Although there is no healing instruction manual, the biggest element of healing is retelling – that is, communication. It works spectacularly when the person you are telling is listening with unbounded compassion. In the anonymous world of crisis lines, I sometimes say: "you can tell the story here if you like – some people find it helps to get it out." And indeed I am often the first person they tell the whole story to.

There is a very interesting thing about memories and retelling them – the fish story phenomenon. Our long-term memory has a feature that when something comes out of it and we speak about it, we hear ourselves speak, and the new version that we have just put into words is what gets re-recorded back in long-term memory. So when people tell a story over and over, for example, about that big fish they caught, the fish gets a bit bigger with each retelling. The speaker really believes the size of the fish each time – it is not a lie, but rather a genuine, false memory. The story creeps away from reality because of the number of times it is retold, not because of the time elapsed since it happened.

For the same reason, when something has never been said before, the first time it comes out is essentially never a false memory. When my friend remembered being raped by her father after a decade, it had been preserved in deep freeze and when it came up, it was being re-experienced verbatim. The memory cannot creep away from reality when it is sealed and never retold.

PROBLEMS WITH THERAPY APPROACHES

I get a different look at how trauma works by talking to many people for a short time, as compared with therapists who talk to a few people over a much longer time. One of my top complaints about the industry is that it has moved away from Freudian-informed techniques in favor of a slew of coping techniques that keep the client in the present and teach them to solve problems practically without getting lost in the past. Freud was discredited on some ideas, but the thrust of his contribution is how past trauma controls a person from an unconscious driver's seat, and that part needs to better inform how therapy is done today.

Coping skills work until they don't, and when you get to the end of their efficacy, it is a scary cliff edge. We need to practice trauma healing in an ongoing way, not just when other approaches fail. We need to get to where we can fall, cry, get up, and be done – all in hours or days instead of months or years. A lot of people I talk to have focused on learning coping skills, which I would rather call *deferring* skills – ways to avoid crying or other expressions of pain in order to get through the day.

A common therapy technique today is bringing people back to the present when they are lost in a triggered state of fear ("You were in danger back then, but you are safe now"). Learning to be fully present in the here and now is of course delightful and powerful, but people are not always safe now, and it is not accurate to assume that. Current fears from past memories can signal actual current danger, in large part because a person who is substantially broken by past trauma will often have a faulty danger detector. Those who can distinguish real from imagined danger can steer towards safety, but those who cannot are rightfully concerned about being in danger more of the time.

Some survivors of trauma who experience triggers and PTSD have very singular triggers. A common scenario is the veteran whose war memories are triggered by gun shots. But a lot of people have more vague sources of triggers stemming from the whole way they were raised or other factors about the environment that were disempow-ering. Those people tend to be in a triggered state a lot of the time because the triggers are unavoidably omnipresent. Listening to people in that place must assume they are right about their fears and other feelings; we cannot dictate "you are safe now."

I feel like a lot of people have complex PTSD like this – the continuous trauma that a person's life is made of, rather than a trauma that is an interruption of life. Some of us (like me) cannot really clearly identify what the "original" trauma is. We supposedly had a nice childhood with no dark secrets or anything that we know of, but yet we are living in a state of high stress all the time, defending against attacks that we cannot see, or being ineffective at moving on in life from the emotional blocks.

As a final point about approaches to trauma therapy, I want to talk about the quest for happiness. Our culture has a blind spot for what happiness and sadness really are. A lot of people in crisis will say, "I just want to be happy – is that too much to ask?" Short answer: yes. We get taught that sadness is bad, and happiness is good and should be the norm at all times. A more informed and realistic view of these things is that both feelings (and all other feelings as well) are tools of expression, and that expression fixes something or corrects an imbalance. Every feeling that wells up is an opportunity to express it and act on it. If we understand our feeling language and have personal power to make changes, each feeling is informative for how we can steer our lives. Sadness leads to crying or some other action that resolves the situation. Happiness helps us steer in a good way, but we cannot be in an elated state continu-ously; that must also return to normal. Pretending to be in constant excitement is valued in our culture, but it is too much to ask for since it is not real. So all feelings are powers of growth, and none should be discouraged as "bad."

Depression is a state of not having a wide range or intensity of feelings. It is not the state of being especially sad. Depression slows growth since we do not have the evidence of feelings as the impetus to steer our lives.

TRAUMA MOUNTAIN

If life is a path in a woods, we cannot always see what lies ahead. If we are carrying a lot of trauma, the path may lead to a seemingly impassable mountain. Catching glimpses of the mountain through the trees may be frightening and cause us to avoid moving forward or try to find another way around. The mountain, which represents trauma from the past in this analogy, is a barrier to moving ahead, as nothing really ever stays in the past. Catching glimpses of the mountain represents being triggered: something comes up which permits us to see the scary thing. Naturally we look away, stay back, and maybe stop moving through life at all.

This analogy and image is something that could come in a dream: often the scary thing in a dream represents part of ourselves that we do not want to face, but the dream is sometimes telling us that we are ready for the trial. Dreams can help us be ready to face big things by changing them into objects that represent the scary thing, such that we do not realize at first what the thing represents. In that way we can bypass the trigger response, and get a more gentle nudge to face it.

Calling a crisis line has some things in common with a dream of this kind. The counselor, by being a support on this path, can make it possible to summon the courage to look at the mountain, even go up to it. In the dream language, the idea is to eventually climb it, which represents the arduous path of healing, but that work does not happen in one call.

Walking towards the mountain with a counselor is risky territory because we can dig up too much at once that we are not ready for and even increase the sense of crisis. So many people I have talked to have verbally wandered around their mountains in ways that give me a definite intuition that something from their past is looming frighteningly and they are not yet talking about it – maybe it was incest or neglect. When I was less experienced I would encourage them forthright to shine a light on the big hurts they were trying to forget, because I was pretty certain that their current suffering would be eased by healing from that trauma. But I found that after building trust with someone, they could be in a very vulnerable state and be so raw and open that any suggestion from me could bypass their normal judgment, and they might go too far at once and then become intensely triggered. This can be life threatening for people considering suicide.

This is why in crisis training, we are usually told not to go there. For a crisis volunteer who does not have credentials and will not see the person again, it is considered dangerous by some to ever go to that territory of digging up the past. One of the reasonable outcomes of a crisis call is to air only the current pains and frustrations and then be referred to a therapist in a setting where they can work on the longer term things.

I remain somewhat non-compliant though, because I still feel that facing the mountain in a moment of suicide crisis is often a risk worth taking; in fact it is frequently the very thing that saves a life. With some more experience, I now say things like: "If you want, you can talk about some of those bad things" or, "Some people find that by telling the story it takes some of the weight off." The more careful way of inviting that retelling helps keep the caller in charge and less likely to go too far out of their comfort zone in a moment of vulnerability.

To clarify, the risks I have been talking about are due to the potentially shocking effect of triggers, so this applies in an early stage of healing where the mountain has not been faced directly before. Later in a healing process, it is possible to bring up more memories with less risk, because the person is already on her way up the mountain and has a better-known course ahead. Within the analogy of this mountain image, my sense is that a person is most likely to take her life in the earlier area of the path before seeing the mountain, because that is the place where no movement is happening. Some sharks have to swim to stay alive, and likewise people need to be moving on our life paths to stay connected to our life force. When we stay in the same place for months or years without support to face the big things, this makes it seem like we will be there forever; there is no point in living if we really did stay there forever. I mean that literally: if a person really is doomed to stay in the same place, death is a better option. But once we accept the mountain is there, that no alternate escape routes exist, and that we have to climb it, then there is movement and thus less risk of suicide.

LISTENER TRIGGERS

Triggers are helpful as a signal of the path forward, but we also naturally want to avoid them. Crisis volunteers can also be triggered by the topics brought up, but we cannot use the time for our own processing. So managing our own state of mind-body activation is an additional challenge beyond listening to the caller. Some volunteers get triggered by suicide, or anger, or a variety of other topics that relate to their past. In order to listen with the most compassion, we need to be in a real and vulnerable state; we cannot robotically distance ourselves and remain effective, so those triggers will most definitely come up.

For me, the main trigger I have experienced is around sexual ease. Being queer and disabled in high school and college effectively locked me out of the dating pool. When someone was polite or friendly in passing, I mistook it as a permanent friendship or romantic interest, only for my hopes to be shattered time after time. Now when I interact with people telling me about their sexual options or that someone wants them, I get triggered. It is the worst when someone talks about cheating or any situation where they go out and hook up with someone, just because they felt like it, as if it is effortless for them. My brain reacts to the unfairness and it has been very hard to see their issues the way they see them.

Getting triggered a bunch of times by this does not constitute healing, but I was able to make progress by talking about it and journaling, with repeated controlled exposure. Some people have talked about the struggle of too much sexual attention and the danger of it. My first automatic reaction is: "At least you're getting attention!" and I block out what they are actually saying. It helped to imagine being wealthy and having people use me for money, or being naive and having people use me for bullying or for copying homework, and was then able to generalize how it feels to be *used*. People get targeted and used for all different things, but it feels lousy regardless of the reason. With practice and attention to these thoughts, my compassion grew enough so that now when someone has struggles with being sexually used, I can let the automatic reaction come and go, take a breath and then see them better from their point of view.

Some volunteers have wanted to be able to avoid calls on certain subjects that trigger them. If I did that I would be missing a growth opportunity and would be avoiding doing the thing that I am encouraging others to do in their paths. We need to accept the hard lessons that comes with this kind of work. Also, if we had hand-offs based on topic, it would be a pretty bad experience for the caller.

Leadership

CIRCLES ORGANIZATIONAL MODEL

My first interaction with Agora was with students. Students in volunteer and paid leadership roles took my application, interviewed me, organized training logistics, sent out all the emails, mentored me, and ran role plays. Students handle organizing shifts, debriefing, escalations (like EMT or police involvement), and many other aspects. After being around a while I was invited to take on some of these roles too. It was eye opening to see how effectively a student club could operate and maintain its momentum for five decades when most volunteers are only there during part of their undergraduate years.

No one noticeably older than college age was anywhere to be seen throughout this on-boarding process until after training started, at which point Molly opened the first training topic, seemingly mid-sentence with no introduction and certainly no fanfare. I did not know who it was leading the exercises at first, and it seemed like it must be someone in a supporting position rather than the director. The reason it felt this way, looking back, is that she really is primarily in a supporting position – that is how she sees her role as director.

The secret to the club's longevity amid high turnover lies in the leadership model: the director supports a core group, who support the rest of the volunteers, who in turn support the rest of the world. It is a pond with ripples flowing outward from a core.

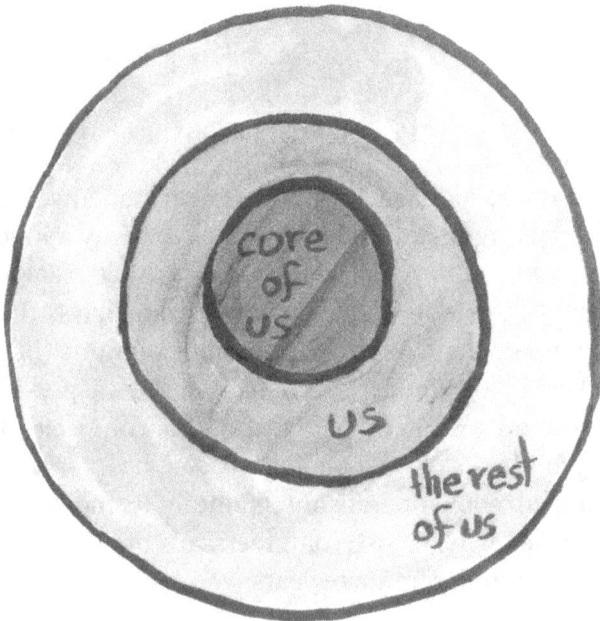

I call this the "circles organizational model," where the leadership, volunteers, and other beneficiaries are all in the same big circle. Here is what I have experienced as the special and essential parts of this model.

- **There is no "they."** Instead of "us" (staff and volunteers) serving "them" (people in crisis), there is just wider circles of us. This standpoint engenders a practice of not looking down at anyone, and remembering that "we" (meaning everyone) can all experience crisis and we all need support. What we do for the world is what we do for each other.

- **Support flows outward, not upward.** In some organizations, you are serving your superiors in a chain of command; even in non-hierarchical and charitable organizations, there is often a sense of credit being claimed by the main leader. At Agora, there is no such elevation of the central people. Appreciation of everyone else is spoken, printed in the newsletters, posted on the wall, invited and repeated often. These appreciations flow outward to the newest people joining the circle. Those more in the core take on more responsibility for doing the appreciation, but it does not entitle them to more attention.

- **Positive support is everywhere,** baked in the culture and into every practice. After I have offered support for a caller or another volunteer, often some other volunteer or staff checks in with me to offer support. Dozens of people have said to call them any time if I need anything.

- **Evaluation is never negative.** There is the assumption that everyone is doing their best, and simultaneously that everyone can always learn more. There is a recognition that some people shine in certain circumstances but that does not become a standard to measure other people against. There has to be judgment about certain volunteers not being ready to take calls, but that is talked about as just "not ready yet."

- **Learning is the purpose.** The entire structure is set up with training first, ongoing self-evaluation, and learning in the role. It is hard to say whether learning is first and service is second, or the other way around, because it is more like service is done within the educational context.

- **There is a path to leadership** and to taking on more roles and responsibilities, so you can advance as much as you want to and can. This brings people into supporting roles in a fairly self-selected way; those who have a drive towards more intense immersion can follow that path. Thus the roles are mostly filled by people who are motivated, not burnt out, and at the point in life where holding that role is the most rewarding; thus they are inspired in the job and most capable of inspiring others.

- **Burdensome work** like fundraising, number crunching, and office tasks are handled more by the director or a paid assistant. There is no delegation of the tedious stuff to people "lower" in the chain. These tasks, though time consuming, have never been highlighted; no one asks for applause for it. To me this is one of the more important but less recognized aspects of true servant leadership.

I do not mean to imply that leaders in the circle model just do assistant work. Molly, who is at the center of Agora, is the voice and navigator. She spends a lot of time reminding people of the values, setting the direction, and resolving anything that goes astray. It is a position of strength. Older experienced people can often see more dimensions of things where younger people might adhere to the surface form. Without Molly, Agora could easily disintegrate into factions, or lose the deeper reasons for things in favor of a legalistic system of rules.

EVALUATIONS

Concerning evaluations being mainly positive and rarely negative, some people are not sold on this idea because it can seem like coddling. A more dominant theory says that you need to know what you have done wrong in order to correct it. We are mostly accustomed to this approach in schools, where tests are graded by counting the wrong answers, subtracting points from 100, and the result shows how far below perfect you are. Also in schools, teachers may write all over student papers in red, defacing them, and bringing focus only to errors.

In a creative writing class that I taught, I ran an experiment where I switched this around, and only evaluated students on what I liked about their writing, saying nothing about negatives. I attached a separate sheet instead of marking on the paper, and made it personal rather than the usual false objectivity about what was "good" and "bad." The comments would be about simple things like correct spelling or neatness, or things I noticed about descriptive language, or parallels, or anything that engages a reader. The result was a dramatic and meaningful involvement in the class. If you step back and think about it, how is a student supposed to improve if the teacher can find nothing of value in their work? A student who wants to succeed might think: "well she didn't like that, so I'll take a stab at something completely different at random and see if she likes that." There is no known direction of improvement in this way. However, if she wrote a paper that would normally be considered "bad" (misspellings, messy, disorganized, etc.) but one aspect was emotionally engaging, and the teacher focuses on that one positive aspect, then this gives the student a direction: Keep doing more like that. One student might be able to improve around a core of emotional engagement, while another might have a core around fantasy character superpowers. Since we are all different, we will write differently, and there does not need to be a measure of how badly we failed to meet a standard.

To me this way needs to be the way we do schools, jobs, volunteer positions, and everything. The adage of learning from mistakes is not quite true. We learn to do things better only by comparing a success and a failure, not just by failing.

REPLICATING THE MODEL

I wanted to replicate the circles model in another nonprofit – an autistic run retreat center called Ocate Cliffs. I have found that it is very difficult to communicate how and why the model works, and I think most people are not accustomed to it. The assumption may be that the leader is supposed to control everything and get credit for it, while others are given delegated tasks, like a typical business. I was not able to replicate it very well.

My fear is that the benefits of the model are hidden; those first looking at Agora may not notice that the leadership model is a core reason for its success. My failure in implementing it elsewhere tells me it is hard to explain with logic; it is more of something you need to feel while working in it. Even long-term Agorans can be at a loss for words to explain how and why they feel so passionately about it. In my interviews, I got a lot of, "It's so great!" and, "I learned a lot," but articulating more about it is hard. My deeper fear then is the model being lost as the world goes in a totally different direction, so that is part of my drive to write about it here.

JUSTICE

I said above that "there is no they," and these four words deserve more exposure. It is subtle yet earth-shattering that no one touching the organization in any way is the "other." Every possible root of violence and injustice involves drawing a line between "legitimate" people and the "other." Racism starts with defining the line between so-called races. The non-profit world is practically based on othering in their attempts to "help" "target-populations." As a person who is routinely othered based on disability, it has been life-changing to be allowed in the organization at all, and treated as equal even though I cannot do a lot of things that most people can.

This principle extends to the way therapeutic interactions are done: there is no behavioral component to the engagement. We do not tell anyone what is right to do. By contrast, in the mainstream of psychology today, behaviorism (the science of and control of behavior) is rampant, and it flourishes only because the industry has labeled certain people as behavior-disordered, which is a form of othering.

The organizational model connects directly with the non-behavioral form of help being offered. Together, these two components promote justice in action.

UNIVERSITY STRUCTURE

Just as the philosophy has proven durable, the structure has not seen much change. Agora is a student club with a professional director, so there are two lines of authority. Agora is one of the 300 clubs chartered by the Student Activities Center (SAC); as such, Agora's student governing board is accountable to SAC. At the same time, Molly is staff in the psychology department, and is accountable to the dean and other structures of the university. Perhaps the balance of power has prevented one party from becoming too controlling, and contributed to its longevity.

EFFECT ON VOLUNTEERS

Agora has been a career launchpad and life-changing experience for so many volunteers.

Meghan, Molly's daughter, grew up surrounded by the Agora community and as such, has a special view of it. Remembering childhood, she says it affected every part of her life: "Agora stuff was supercool! There were parties, nice people, it was beautiful!" She feels lucky to be exposed to a model of how people treat each other so well from a young age. She went on to volunteer and help run trainings.

Meghan explained some of the deeper effects to me, which she reflected on during her time working theater gigs and scraping by on restaurant work. "You have no choice but to feel what the customers feel." In other words, she was able to talk customers down when they were irate, or connect to them about anything. She could more easily figure out where people are coming from in tense theater situations, by empathizing and hearing their feelings. "Why wouldn't you want everyone in your life to feel more seen and heard? It's not about you."

When she went into teaching, Agora's lasting lessons helped her build relationships with students. Particularly post-pandemic, she is using this background to help them practice empathy and rebuild communication abilities that faltered in the lost time of the pandemic.

She also echoes a faith in humanity that is palpable among volunteers: "If there is at least one person constantly there, it gives me hope for the world."

Here are a few more observations from other volunteers – just a tiny sample showing the far reaching effects of the ripples:

- David and Diane were volunteers in the early 1970s. They met through Agora and later got married. This is not like an office workplace where relationships are discouraged; instead, people bring their whole selves and often find deep friendships and soulmates. David says: "Agora touched my heart and made me want to go out in the world and touch other people's hearts too."

- Another recent volunteer says training was really hard, but she became a whole new person. "My worldview changed and I became someone I like a lot more. Random people start talking to me since they see I am a listener."

- Stephanie says she stuck with Agora long term because of being a part of the community. "Joining with people of the same mindset was energy giving. It became part of my being. The new way of approaching support matched my instinct, and the training made that instinct real."

- Dasie credits the Agora model with helping her talk with friends and everyone else non-judgmentally.

- Francesca recalls from her involvement in the 1980s: "I loved my time at Agora. I learned so much about how to interact with those in crisis. Some of my dearest friendships were made during those years. Professionally, I ended up working for 20 years in mental health after getting my psych degree from UNM. I am now a high school English teacher where I am part of a suicide prevention team. My Agora training has been a significant influence in my life professionally and personally. I am thrilled that Agora still exists and I hope it will continue for decades to come."

- Dr. James Walker, now a research therapist, got a start at Agora and says it "gave me a solid foundation in being a good communicator. I learned how to ask thoughtful questions, not shallow questions. In classes, I felt ahead of my peers who didn't have that experience."

Molly has contributed as a volunteer to various efforts since childhood, and feels it is an anchor in her life. Getting letters about how Agora volunteering profoundly changed people's lives helps her to avoid getting overly caught up in the day-to-day issues.

Autonomy

EXISTENTIALISM

Imagine looking over the edge of a cliff in a place where it would be easy to fall. Or imagine a tenth-floor balcony with a flimsy railing. In these situations we might become light-headed or feel that our footing is unsure, even though we are standing on a solid surface just like anywhere else. What is the actual reason for the angst over this? Maybe no one else is there, so there is no danger of being pushed, and there is little chance of accidentally falling. But we can still feel angst or even terror over the fact that we ourselves have the power to make the decision to jump. We have fear of our own power, even when there is no fear of the inherent danger in the situation. This is *existential power*, essentially the only power that no one can take away from us.

DEFINING AUTONOMY

I am defining "autonomy" here to mean reasonable levels of self determination, the power and capacity to make non-coerced decisions, and being the person at the steering wheel of your own life.

We need autonomy, and in an ideal trajectory from childhood to adulthood, we would get more and more power in a gradual and safe sequence. We start as a toddler in a sandbox – figuratively and sometimes literally – able to move only within small boundaries where we cannot get hurt. The sandbox grows as we do, mainly because we push against those boundaries and our parents allow them to widen. One of the hardest questions as parents is whether to allow a child the freedom they want, or curtail it for their safety. It is a hard question because the answer changes constantly, or at least it should change constantly, so it is a problem that has to get brought up and solved over and over, in tension with the child. A child is often ahead in her mind, more advanced inside than the parents are willing to see and accept.

Some teens feel smothered and treated like young children by their parents. Most teens feel that sometimes, but a few are so restricted in their autonomy that it feels like they are in prison.

THE CAGE

One way to understand that feeling of imprisonment is to imagine yourself in a wire cage that is being gradually lowered into water, so slowly that you might not notice it at first. But as it goes lower you figure out what's happening, try to strategize, but there is no way out, and then you start to panic as you are faced with inevitable drowning. However, it is so gradual that you're still alive after exhausting yourself from panic. You may find yourself alive day after day in this cage that represents inevitable death. Your thoughts become consumed with needing the torture to end, and you just keep living in this state of wanting to die as the way out.

Even when all autonomy has been taken away (or at least from our perception in the situation) we all still have existential power. Taking our own life is our last and greatest power. Our need for autonomy is so great that we will ultimately use that power if all other power has been taken away.

The cage metaphor is not the only one that describes a powerless feeling. Some people feel more like they are flying or falling, and the important aspect of that feeling is that there is no ground – nothing solid in life, and nothing reliable to trust. Others feel swept in a current or abandoned in a desert or a void. Others feel an immense weight or suffocation.

The cage metaphor

KINDS OF AUTONOMY

In my listening work I have found that a very common experience of a majority of people thinking about suicide is lack of autonomy. It is not about how lonely you are, or how many bad experiences you've been through, but whether you have the power to act – to open the door of the cage and get out. Even people who have lives that look perfect from the outside – wealth and academic awards and friends and talents – can still be lacking in that power.

Sometimes a disability reduces autonomy. Sometimes it is connected to overly controlling parents. Even older teens and college students sometimes have their phones taken away by parents, who misidentify the need for the phone as an unhealthy addiction. In reality the phone is a main way to reach people: no phone, no connections. Those not with their parents can have a similar situation with an abusive partner, and not have the money to make a change.

The autonomy that we all need includes:

- freedom of physical movement
- control of physical and sexual boundaries
- freedom of association
- freedom to think, study, and make our own conclusions about beliefs
- access to communication and being heard
- freedom from internalized oppression stemming from threats based on identity or beliefs
- freedom to die

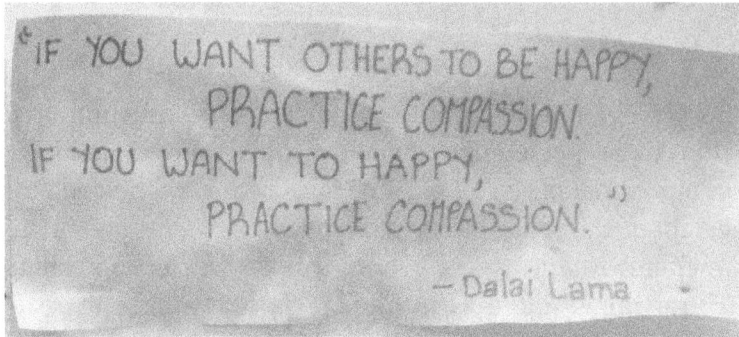

"IF YOU WANT OTHERS TO BE HAPPY, PRACTICE COMPASSION. IF YOU WANT TO HAPPY, PRACTICE COMPASSION."

— Dalai Lama

NERVOUS SYSTEM

In "The Body Keeps the Score" (2014), Dr. Bessel Van der Kolk describes physiology research about the nervous system which puts the cage metaphor into actual measurable terms. There are three distinct kinds of nervous system activation, not just a continuum. The most common and least extreme type of activation is social: when we sense a threat we move closer to other people for protection and to tie our emotional regulation to theirs with high levels of emotional communication. When this is unsuccessful or the threat is too great, the fight-or-flight response in the nervous system is activated; this involves different nerves and a much higher state of arousal. When this fails, the third and most extreme kind of activation occurs, which is dissociating and dialing down the energy consumed by the body. The third level is like playing dead – a person can be still and vacant-looking in this state.

That book is highly recommended if you want to understand more about trauma from a research perspective.

WHAT TO AVOID

Some less effective interventions involve attempting to prevent the person from suicide by physical restraint, logic, or emotional pleas. All of these take away power, which can heighten the sense of crisis. So even platitudes like "Hang in there!" and "It gets better" can be felt as controlling. Those things indicate the helper is not willing to really listen, so it cuts off agency of communication. Emotional pleas like "your mom/sister/son/dog/etc. would never forgive you" take away agency over identity and beliefs. Even the word "intervention" suggests that the helper is active and the person being helped is passive, so just starting with that word choice risks doing things that restrict autonomy.

WAYS TO HELP BUILD AUTONOMY

When talking with someone in a crisis, the type of help that works depends on the state of the nervous system at the time. Or another way to think of it is using the submerging cage metaphor. If the cage is just now being perceived as a problem, then the person can likely connect with a listener. But if the cage is almost completely submerged and the person is gasping for breath, that calls for a different kind of help because the nervous system is in a whole different state. The most important thing to keep in mind is that there is no effective social communication or rationality or problem solving when a person is in the higher elevated states. The panic has to be dealt with first. A common mistake made when helping people who are in those elevated states is to say things like, "Well yelling and pacing won't solve the problem!" It is a mistake because we cannot redirect someone else into a solution-oriented mode when they are in panic.

A helper has to keep a variety of help levels in mind so we do not accidentally attempt the wrong kind of support for the current mental state. Following is a way of categorizing helpful things that one can do. I have mixed together things that a crisis counselor can do as well as family members or others.

Help with physical safety

Physical help means ensuring the person in crisis is not in any current danger to life or health. They may be requested to move away from a weapon or other means of suicide, go to a hospital, or just go somewhere else. If any of these needs are critical for the person, then the other aspects of crisis are not as important, so these often need to be addressed first.

This type of help has the most potential to clash with the person's need for autonomy, since in some cases there can be forced removal of weapons or forced hospitalization. In order to save a life, it may be a good idea to violate the person's autonomy, but that violation will not be forgotten and will contribute to crisis at other levels. So it is essential to request, not try to order something, and to engage in whether something is a good idea rather than give absolute advice.

When it comes to running away, I have talked to teens about that, and some may think I am encouraging breaking the law or getting into danger. But if they are already in high danger, running away could do some positive things: One, to escape one danger and possibly leave them with other dangers (but less); and two, to get more people involved. The other people could be friends and their parents, school principals. or even police. Also the benefits of taking *some* action (even if it is not the best idea) cannot be underestimated. The experience of deciding something to do and following through can be very empowering and sets the stage for deciding more steps after that. Many times a person in crisis can only handle making a decision to do one thing.

Hospitalization done on an emergency basis is almost never a good experience, and has the potential to traumatize someone more than the alternatives, and turn them off to considering help in that way for a very long time. When I talk to people about medical and emergency kinds of help, they have often had a spike of fear and it creates a sudden wall between them and myself; even the suggestion of maybe going inpatient can shatter trust of the listener. So it is important to balance this option with other alternatives, even including running away.

Moving to a new location can help a person think straight, and regain selfhood, in cases where the home environment is so toxic that they have lost a sense of who they are. If home is a place where sexual boundaries are routinely violated, for example, the person is on 24-hour high alert in the very place where they should have the most safety. There is no real rest, and therefore no way to clear one's mind and make good decisions.

Legal and financial help

This kind of help ties in with physical help, and includes being able to afford to move, to have a place to live to escape abuse, and to file a restraining order or a police report of a crime. It is easy for me to get really involved in feelings and stories from the past, and forget to check in on these things. A crisis counselor usually cannot do much in this area except to bring up some options. But a friend with a car or a place to stay can be a huge enabler of safety.

One of the elements of partner abuse is preventing the victim from leaving by ensuring they do not have money or transportation, and are isolated. This pattern also occurs quite a lot with teens whose parents might not be considered abusers in any legal sense, but they are trying to "protect" the teen from the world by ensuring they do not have money, means of communication, or transportation.

Help for panic

Sometimes the first thing that happens on a call, before any words can be found, is directly addressing a state of panic. Ways to do this on the phone include breathing slowly together, or asking the person to describe sights, sounds, or anything else physical in their environment. This is grounding and connecting. People in a panic cannot lead the conversation (rational language may not be fully there), so in these cases the helper has to lead more strongly. If you are with someone in person, depending on your relationship, you can touch, or even hold and massage someone to ground them in that way.

Coping help

There are times when a short-term plan to get through a hard day or an anxiety-inducing event can be the right thing. I think of coping as steeling the psyche for a while, while deferring actual healing. It only helps you last a little longer and the coping strategies do not tend to be a lasting solution. It is hard to suggest a coping strategy for someone else, but most people know what has worked for them.

While this is one tool available, a lot of people have run out of strategies by the time they call a crisis line. They may say, "I've tried all my coping strategies and they are not working any more." From what I hear from people in crisis, coping strategies are the dominant form of help offered by their systems of support, and I think we are failing people in that way. Coping as a long-term strategy is basically encouraging a kind of "strength" to handle adversity after adversity without any change in the situation and without building the capacity to grow.

Helping by listening

Listening is the bread and butter of crisis counseling, as was spelled out at the beginning of the book. It can be a direct repetition of what was heard, and can add emotion words. It can involve guessing and checking for understanding. It is so effective partly because it keeps the person in crisis in power and respects their autonomy. I may be very curious about many things about someone who is calling, but I do not ask about things just because of my curiosity; I only ask if I sense that talking about something will help them make sense of it.

Listening can be a gift of autonomy. When someone is struggling with personal power and has no opportunity to be heard within their network, a crisis counselor can say almost nothing; the absence of judgment and competition, along with the open space within which to express oneself is like fresh air, a feeling of empowerment.

Helping with universal truths

A "universal truth" is a statement like "everyone needs love" or "no one deserves that kind of treatment." It is easy to confuse universals with platitudes, like "it will get better." The latter is not a universal truth; it is more like an empty wish. When we hear a universal truth, it clicks into place. It may be something we resist believing, but the power of a simple, true statement has a way of pushing down our walls of resistance. For example, someone might think she does not deserve love, but when she hears it stated in a universal way, it raises an internal dilemma of how she got to feeling that way even though she knows it is true in the abstract.

We have to be careful to avoid minimizing statements, such as "everyone feels that way sometimes." It may be true and almost universal, but a statement like that is not relevant to the crisis at hand. It can be heard as minimizing the depth of the problem. A minimizing truth quells feelings (as if saying "don't feel that"), while a well-chosen universal truth ignites outrage or other strong feelings. As another example, suppose someone was fired from a job. Here are two possible responses:

- "You're not alone – lots of people have been fired from something." This is true but it can feel restricting, and can make a person feel more stuck (less autonomy).

- "For many people, being fired can be a deep loss and destroy your confidence." This is also true but more expansive, and can make a person feel more heard and connected in a common plight (more autonomy).

The universals help with feeling connected to humanity in a way that opens up options. It also helps stir up awareness of internalized oppression and false self-imposed limitations.

Helping with permanent healing

By permanent healing, I mean the process of surfacing trauma, expressing it, and reconnecting with the life force – the stuff of successful long-term therapy. This is contrasted with merely coping, or getting through today.

Doing a little of the big healing work in a moment of crisis may be counter-intuitive. People might say that if a person in crisis is standing on a bridge about to jump, asking them if their mother treated them well twenty years ago is beside the point. Training in crisis counseling focuses a lot more on the immediate situation and discourages anything that might be opening a can of worms, that might be re-traumatizing, or that might be beyond the skill of the listener.

Nevertheless, time and time again, I have found that opening the door to the big healing is precisely what helps with the immediate crisis. If we can listen compassionately enough to evoke the connection between a person's original trauma and the current situation, it illuminates the path to the mountain, and people can feel a sudden surge of strength to stay alive through touching on the past trauma.

So many people believe that forgetting painful things is possible and is a good way to move forward. I tell them it is okay to address it and that healing is possible, but that forgetting is probably not possible. Many times it has only taken a few minutes for people to accept that they will never really forget and they start asking how they can heal. I tell them that retelling the stories is vital, either to me right now, or in journals, or artwork, or music. A tiny practice in a moment of extreme vulnerability can open a flood of feelings that is so welcome after years of energy spent trying to keep the floodgates closed. That puts healing in their own hands, which is a deep kind of autonomy.

ANONYMITY

One form of autonomy that crisis lines are good at respecting, but the other systems are less effective at, is anonymity and privacy. People need to say things and know that what they say will not cause them to be taken to involuntary hospitalization, or get around to their family or others in their life. So many people I have talked to are absolutely not going to tell their secrets to anyone, even in-person counselors. They do not trust anyone to respect their privacy. Even at Agora, people often need to confirm "Is this really confidential?" The need to speak openly with no consequences is so basic to being human; those who do not have such an opportunity among people they know can use an anonymous crisis line for the purpose. They can use a false name and refuse to give contact information, and that is fine.

I want to recognize also that some people will not even call a confidential line because they do not believe we are truly confidential no matter what we say.

TEENS

Teens have a special need for anonymity because they often do not get the privacy they need. In the worst case, they may have rules in the house about the doors staying open, their internet activity tracked, and so on. It is supposedly for their own protection, but a lot of the time, when it gets extreme, it is a teen girl and her father is getting hyperbolic about sexual risks in a way that makes it seem like he is projecting his own sexual issues.

The invasion of privacy that prevents people from speaking openly is sometimes far worse than the actual topic they might need to talk about. If they want to talk to any other adult (school counselor or teacher), those people are often required or feel obligated to tell the parents what was said. But the parents may be part of the problem. Even if the parents are okay at parenting, a teen's life is inherently wound up in parental relationships; one of the primary jobs of adolescence is separating from them.

I am convinced that the lack of guaranteed private communication is one of the biggest risk factors for teen suicide. Without being able to express, movement in healing is blocked.

Sometimes when adults learn about a teen crisis, they crack down on autonomy, which makes it much worse. Molly told me about someone who was only keeping herself alive because she was in a school theater production – her only lifeline – but when they found out she was suicidal, they took her out of school. They could not hear and understand that having choices and opportunities is essential to her life force and instead assumed that cracking down and forcing "help" on her would more likely address the suicidal thoughts.

THEIR AUTONOMY VERSUS MY LIABILITY

When someone is considering suicide, a helper has choices about what kind of approach to take. Even if you believe that people should have the legal and moral right of suicide, most of the time that is not what they really want. They almost always want to find another way out.

When the basic problem is lack of autonomy, there are a lot of ways to help, but all effective ways to help involve one major thing in common: honoring that agency, including honoring their existential power. That means we might not always do everything possible to prevent their death, but also we do not just do nothing.

What should be done when someone is already dying while on the phone with a crisis line? In general the first course of action (at Agora and elsewhere) is to call the appropriate local police or ambulance response system – but why? Suppose the person in crisis dialed 988 instead of 911 because they specifically did not want a rescue. Should we not respect that decision? The accepted answer to that question is that we do not always honor that level of autonomy in that case because the person reached out for help, and we can conclude that at least some part of them wants to be saved. People are usually of two or more minds in these circumstances; they say they want to die and at the same time, they call for help or even say they want to live. Both are true. When you are in that terrifyingly submerging cage, getting out or dying both feel like acceptable options.

Molly attended a panel discussion on suicide escalation in crisis centers, in which questions like these were being discussed. Molly is unusual in her insistence on caller autonomy, and prefers to engage and talk for as long as it takes without escalation. She believes that calling for help is warranted, but if at all possible the caller should make their own decision. One of the scenarios on this panel was what to do if we have no name or location information, and therefore could not send help. Every other panelist said they would tell the person to call 911, then hang up on them in order to basically force them to call 911 for rescue. Molly said she would stay on, because the person can change their mind right up to the last second. Allowing that person to retain their existential power to the very end is most likely necessary for them to be able to make the decision to keep living.

Learning

"EVERYTHING WE DO IS TRAINING"

Molly's favorite part of Agora is training, and she says that what we do for volunteers is just as important as helping callers. Towards the end of her career she notes that her main contribution has been measured by the growth in volunteers. They sometimes write and express how the training was profound and instrumental in their careers after college. Many of them say it helped them stay grounded in the most fundamental part of being in any helping role – connection with people and listening to them – when they were faced with many other competing ideas and demands in their jobs. It was the best training on any topic that I have ever attended.

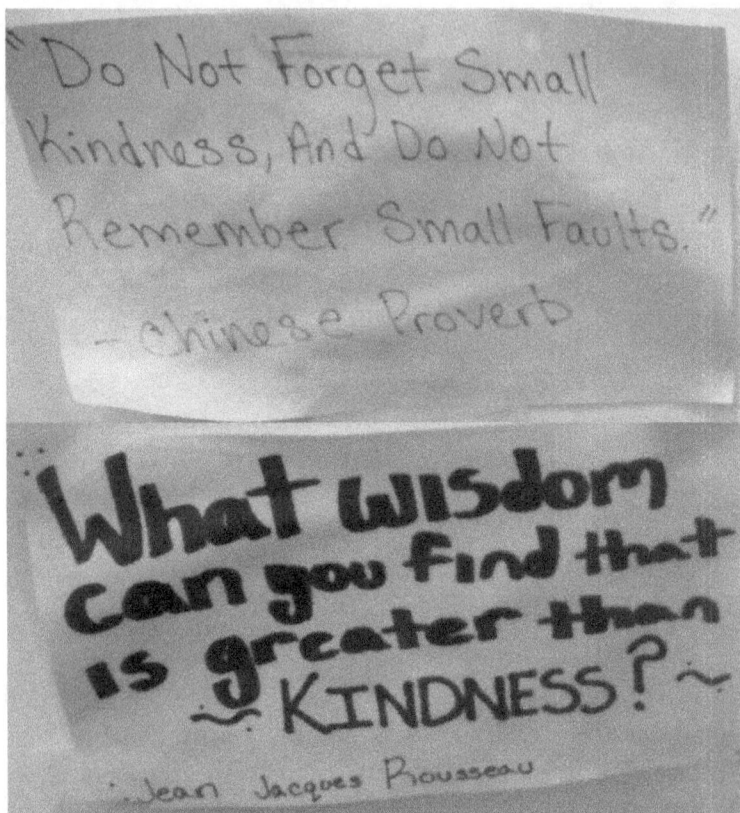

"Do Not Forget Small Kindness, And Do Not Remember Small Faults."
— Chinese Proverb

What wisdom can you find that is greater than KINDNESS?
— Jean Jacques Rousseau

She inherited and expanded the training from predecessors, and from researching other crisis centers. The result is unique to Agora. Everything she does in the 40 hours of initial training time is focused on what she has observed people need to do the work; not a moment is boilerplate or dry. There is always a reason.

Because of the model of student leadership, she does not wing it or work only from private notes; instead she has formalized parts of the training so that others can train. The part of training that needs the most involvement from others is role playing, which I will explain below. There is a clear method to the process that has been proven through experience, and each volunteer first experiences it in their initial training, then often later as a trainer-in-training, then with additional experience as a lead in role plays.

The rest of this chapter is mainly a collection of some of the training exercises that Molly provided. Taken as a whole, along with some lecture topics, they provide ways to learn compassion.

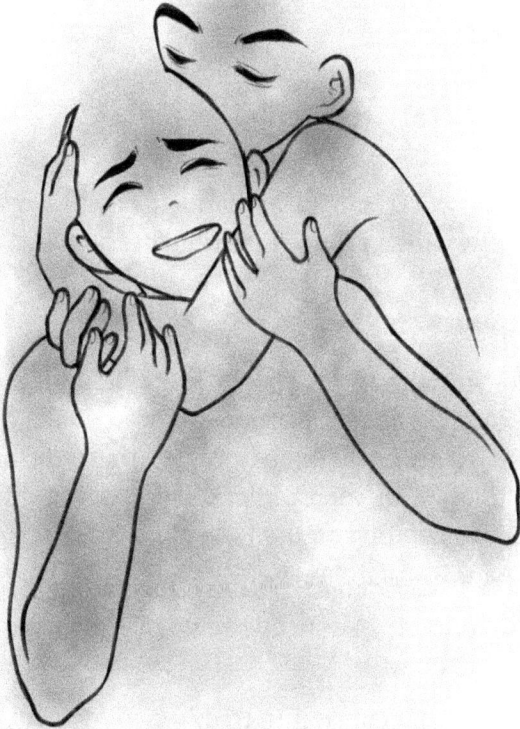

Drawing for "Perception" exercise

PERCEPTION

This exercise exposes how different people see different aspects of things. Look at this drawing of two people. How do you interpret it, and how does it make you feel?

Many volunteers will see the positive aspects of love and affection, but it is also possible to interpret it as a strangling and showing desperation. Often what we choose to see reflects on our biases as much as what is actually there.

After identifying your personal reaction, share with others to learn about as many interpretations as you can.

IDENTIFYING FEELINGS

This written exercise can be handed out to work through individually, with a group reflection afterwards.

Handout:

What do you think are the feelings behind these statements? Read them over to yourself, try to make them come alive, and write down the feeling(s) that you believe are being expressed in each remark. The answers may sometimes vary depending on the tone of voice.

Example: "I just found out my husband's been seeing another woman!" Your answers might include shock, anger, and dismay.

- "I wish I hadn't called him that."

- "I just got a big pay raise!"

- "I don't know. I just can't seem to pull myself together."

- "I was always fighting with my father, and now he's dead."

- "My parents will kill me if they find out I'm pregnant!"

- "That damned kid of mine has been smoking pot again!"

- "I keep trying to explain to my mother that I want to live my own life, but she's so pigheaded!"

- "I feel miserable about failing my finals, after all the money my folks paid out."

- "They've gone off and left me all alone."

- "I don't know how I'm going to manage now that my husband is dead."

- "...so that's my situation. What should I do?"

- "I haven't heard from my son since he left for California a month ago. He's always kept in touch with us before, telephoning or writing. I can't understand what's wrong this time."

SAME FEELINGS, DIFFERENT SITUATION

The facilitator gives the group a potentially charged situation that someone might have, without giving hints about how they feel. For example, someone calls in after having an abortion, or someone calls in because her family is moving her to a new school. In pairs or groups, share what feelings that person might have about the situation. Then find a time in your life when *you* had those same kinds of feelings, even if you have never been in that situation.

As an example using the recent abortion, the group might list feelings like:

- freedom and relief mixed with doubt

- guilt, shame

- sense of lost possibility

Other experiences that a group could list, which evoked similar feelings for them:

- refusing a job promotion

- the death of my abusive great-aunt

- shooting a bird when I was in middle school

The exercise shows how we can empathize without a directly parallel experience. We can hear about problems that we do not have ourselves, but our other experiences can help us make the connection to theirs because we have *felt* some of the same things.

STEREOTYPING

The facilitator tapes four or five blank poster-sized sheets to the wall, and writes broad categories of people as their titles. Some categories you can choose are: Elderly; Christians; Men; People with Mental Illness.

Circulate and write any qualities you can think of that society associates with those people. For example, for the Elderly poster, participants might write "slow," "waste of space," or "don't understand technology." Do not write your own beliefs, but just things that you believe are positive or negative stereotypes in society.

Following this, discuss as a group:

- What is it like to be in one of the categories when you reach out in crisis, knowing that the volunteer on the other end of the phone call might hold some of these negative views?

- Have you held back because of stereotypes about you?

This exercise puts us in touch with those who may have more or different categories than what we have, and shows how easy it is to run with unexamined biases.

HOT TOPICS

This exercise has three parts.

Part 1: Power words

The group counts off 1, 2, 1, 2, etc. creating two equal-sized groups. The "ones" stand in an inner circle facing out while the "twos" stand in an outer circle facing in. Match up with a person in the other circle one to one, and create enough space to not be distracted by neighbors.

The facilitator will give a single word. If you are in the inner circle, speak for three whole minutes about your thoughts and feelings around the word. Do not share information about an article or book you have read or a show you have seen – just your own thoughts and feelings. If you are in the outer circle, stay silent and just listen.

After the three (long!) minutes, switch and the person in the outer circle shares their thoughts and feelings about the same word while the other listens silently.

The first word is FRIEND.

After the two rounds of three minutes, the circles shift one to the right, so you have a new partner. The facilitator gives the next word, repeating the exercise, switching which circle starts each time.

The facilitator will give additional prompt words, increasing in intensity, four in total. The more intense words could be topics that are more intimate, more embarrassing, or potentially triggering.

Part 2: Relaxation

In the second part, you will have the opportunity to relax and become mindful of any tension that the exercise brought to mind. With the lights dim, silently reflect on what this experience has been like for you. Close your eyes. Get in touch with how you feel now. Where is the tension in your body? Release it. Breathe slowly and deeply, concentrate on your breathing. Listen to the sound of your breathing. When you exhale, exhale tension, and inhale relaxation. Think back to how you felt when you arrived. What were your thoughts and feelings when you entered this room? How did you feel when other people came in or when you came in and saw the others? How do you feel now? Where is the tension in your body? Release it. Think about the exercise you just did. Think about the different words: friend, ... Explore your different responses to the different words, and your partners' responses. What words were more difficult to share? Which words were the easiest to talk about? How was the silence for you?

Part 3: Debriefing

A debriefing conversation in groups or with the whole group is done, using these questions:

- Were you able to stay in the here and now?

- Which words were the least comfortable?

- Which words were the most comfortable?

- Which did you prefer, sharing first or second?

- How were the silences for you?

- Which was easier, being silent or being verbal?

- How did it feel to have someone listen to you non-judgmentally?

- How do you think this exercise might be similar to work on the phone?

- How was it to share so personally with someone you might not have known before?

- Did the words test or reveal your values, or the values of the other person?

Summary

This exercise can be done early in training when people do not know each other. It helps to understand how someone might feel calling to talk about personal issues with a stranger.

SECRETS

The facilitator hands out small squares of paper. Write down a secret about yourself, without a name. You can alter your handwriting to keep it anonymous. Give time in silence to maintain a solemn atmosphere while doing this. Fold the paper and place into a hat. The facilitator then shakes up the papers and redistributes them at random. In turns, read the paper you received out loud to everyone, as if it was your own secret. Then say how you feel about this secret (how you believe the author would feel, that is).

Here are a few examples of secrets that have been shared:

- My parents were both alcoholic. (Feelings: I'm frustrated about losing so much time and feel alone.)

- I was raped when I was in high school. (Feelings: I am angry that no one believed me and nothing got fixed.)

- I still wet the bed sometimes. (Feelings: I feel so embarrassed.)

After the readings, discuss these questions: What was it like to write a secret and place it in the hat, not knowing what would happen with it? What was it like hearing your secret read aloud? Were the feelings they said accurate? How did it feel hearing the same or similar secret revealed by someone else? Did the group's reaction to your secret make you feel more or less shame about it?

This powerful exercise shows that we all have shame surrounding some secret, and that we are not alone. Often we feel we are the only one with that shame, but hearing others with a similar secret makes a connection. Each one of us might have a reason to call a crisis line; it is not just "other people" that have problems and need to call.

HELPFUL RESPONSES

This written exercise helps us consider what we might say for different hypothetical situations.

Handout:

The following paragraphs are things that a person might say to you on a call. In each situation, imagine that you are hearing this in a conversation and you want to help by saying the right thing. For each example, write the next thing that you would say. Write only one or two sentences and don't take a lot of time to think it over. Compare and discuss your responses with the group.

- A 41 year-old woman says to you: "Last night Joe got really drunk and he came home late and we had a big fight. He yelled at me and I yelled back and then he hit me really hard! He broke a window and the TV set too! It was like he was crazy. I just don't know what to do."

- A 36 year-old man tells you: "My neighbor really makes me mad. He's always over here bothering us or borrowing things that he never returns. Sometimes he calls us late at night after we've gone to bed and I really feel like telling him to get lost."

- A 15 year-old girl tells you: "I'm really mixed up. A lot of my friends stay out really late and do things their parents don't know about. They always want me to come along and I don't want them to think I'm chicken or something, but I don't know what would happen if I did go."

- A 35 year old mother says: "My Maria is a good girl. She's never been in trouble, but I worry about her. Lately she wants to stay out later and later and sometimes I don't know where she is. She just had her ears pierced without asking me! And some of the friends she brings home – well I've told her again and again to stay away from that kind."

- A 43-year old man says: "I feel really awful. Last night I got drunk and I don't even remember what I did. This morning I found out that the screen of the TV is busted and I think that I probably did it, but my wife isn't even talking to me. I don't think I'm an alcoholic you know, cause I can go for weeks without drinking. But this has got to change."

- A 49 year-old unemployed teacher tells you: "My life just doesn't seem worth living any more. I'm a lousy father. I can't get a job. Nothing good ever happens to me. Everything I try to do turns rotten. Sometimes I wonder whether it's worth it."

PRIVILEGE WALK

Everyone lines up in a straight line, such as along the edge of a path or the wall of a large room. The facilitator reads some statements that might or might not apply to you. For each statement, take a step forward if it applies to you. Each statement is about some form of privilege.

Here are some statements that can be used:

- I have access to transportation that will get me everywhere I need to go.

- I can update my wardrobe with new clothes to match current styles.

- People do not assume that I am unintelligent based on my dialect.

- My decision to go or not to go to college was not based entirely on financial constraints.

- I have a safe and reliable place where I can study.

- People know how to pronounce my name.

- I know that the police and other state authorities are there to protect me.

- I can expect to see many students and professors of my race on campus.

- I can go to a store or spend money knowing that no one will be suspicious of me.

- Most of the time I am able to surround myself with people who share a common or collective history, who speak the same language that I do, and who understand my culture.

- I am allowed to vote.

- No one ever tells me to speak a particular language or to get out of "their" country.

- I can use public facilities like restrooms and locker rooms without fear of verbal abuse, assault, or arrest.

- My gender is an option on legal forms.

- Strangers don't ask me how I have sex.

- I can enter public spaces without being sexually harassed.

- I feel comfortable going somewhere alone or going on a date with someone new; I don't have to fear violence.

- People do not often make unsolicited comments about my body.

- I can go to new places knowing that I will be able to move through the space.

- When I feel unwell or unable to do something, people do not often say that I'm faking it or tell me to just suck it up.

- I am able to enter new situations without fear of debilitating anxiety, embarrassment, harassment, or violence.

- One or both of my parents graduated from college.

- I attended summer camps growing up.

- I have immediate family members who are doctors, lawyers, or work in a degree-required profession.

- My family never had to move due to financial inabilities.

- If I walk into a business and ask to speak to the person "in charge" I will usually see a person of my race.

- School and work are not in session during the major religious holidays that I celebrate.

- I almost always feel comfortable with people knowing my sexual orientation.

After reading these or other similar questions, the group will have spread with those who have had relatively higher privilege out in front. It helps us think about privilege in ways we might not have considered. In particular, having a privilege can seem like second nature, and we may not be aware of it. On the other hand, those who do not have the privilege are constantly reminded of the disparity.

Agora stopped doing this exercise because of the way it puts a spotlight on the person who ends up closest to the starting line, and everyone else notices that she (usually a she) is the least privileged and they may make guesses about her family of origin or make other judgments.

REFLECTION AND SUMMARY

One person is "it," and sits in front of the room facing the others. She invents a "problem" and talks about it for three to four minutes. This can be an imaginary problem or one based on a real situation unknown to the group.

Everyone else then writes down in their notebook what they would reflect back to the speaker. It is important that they write down *exactly* what they would say, word for word, for their reflection.

After a short quiet time for writing, go around the room and read what each person wrote.

Purpose

It quickly becomes apparent that hearing only three or four minutes of a problem produces an amazing amount of material. The variety of reflections posed by the participants reveal that there are many different themes that could be reflected – and many important subtleties in how to word those reflections. What each person chooses to reflect on might also reveal something important about that person. This shows there is no perfect reflection – it is relational and depends on both parties. It is an art.

MASLOW'S HIERARCHY OF NEEDS

The facilitator presents and reviews Maslow's "hierarchy of needs" as shown here:

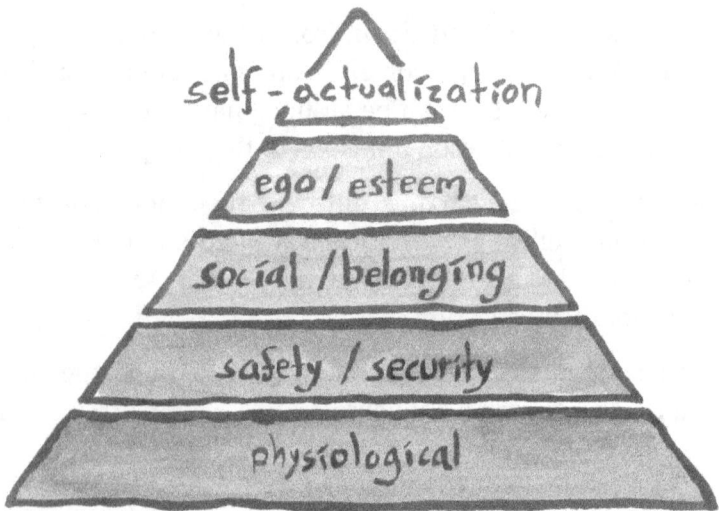

Individually in writing, or in small groups, identify the need or needs being expressed by each caller in the statements below.

- My husband and I are fighting and I've left my house with the kids.

- I'm new in town and want to know how to meet people.

- My girlfriend just broke up with me.

- My dad has been acting "funny" around me.

- I feel really angry at my best friend because she has a new friend.

- My wife died last year and I don't feel like doing anything.

- My son doesn't like it that I call him so much.

- The kids in my class laugh at me.

- I don't like how I feel around a lot of people.

- I'm frightened because my husband is out drinking.

- My 15-year-old is out with some kids I don't approve of.

- I lost my job and don't know how I'm going to feed my kids.

- My ex-boyfriend is telling all kinds of lies about me at school.

- Where can I go to find a job?

- Who in town can help with utility bills?

This exercise helps connect the dots – getting below the level of what people say to the level of feelings and needs.

LOSS

Participants each get 16 squares of paper, 4 of each color. Write one item on each square using these categories:

- On the green squares: Write four different relationships you have.

- On the yellow squares: Write four different possessions of yours.

- On the blue squares: Write four different goals you aspire to.

- On the pink squares: Write four different hobbies you enjoy.

The facilitator then reads aloud the following instructions, representing losses.

- Give me any one square (15 remaining)

- Give me any one Goal (14 remaining)

- Give me any one Possession (13 remaining)

- OK, now I'm going to take one Goal (12 remaining)

- Give me a Relationship (11 remaining)

- Give me a Hobby (10 remaining)

- OK, now I'm going to pick any two squares (8 remaining)

- Now you give me any two squares one of which must be a relationship (6 remaining)

- I choose one square (5 remaining)

- You give me one square (4 remaining)

- I take one square (3 remaining)

- Now turn to someone next to you, close your eyes and let them pick any two squares (1 remaining)

After all this, discuss as a group these questions:

- What was the experience like for you?

- What kinds of feelings did you experience? What kinds of behaviors?

- What kinds of losses gave you the most distress? (gave away card, had card taken, etc.)

- What did it feel like as losses accumulated?

This exercise helps us experience various kinds of losses, and multiple losses, which are a common ingredient in any crisis situation.

RIDES MODEL

The R.I.D.E.S intervention model is a flexible and adaptable way to introspect on the natural progression of problem solving. It consists of five stages. These stages are not rigidly separate, but are interrelated in a process that often flows back and forth as more information is shared. R. I. D. E. S. stands for:

- "R" Rapport

- "I" Identifying the problem

- "D" Dealing with feelings

- "E" Exploring alternatives

- "S" Summary and closing

When we consider the RIDES sequence of conversation stages, it helps us avoid getting ahead of ourselves. We do not need to launch in on alternatives before we have gotten into feelings, but also we might not ask about feelings immediately until we have built a little rapport and trust. When we are not getting very deep in one of the stages, it is easy to just move on – especially if the counselor is nervous about silence or seemingly unproductive talk, but often silence means we need to go back a step or try other ways to get deeper into the step before going to the next step.

Credit: The model was based on one developed by David Switzer.

ROLE PLAYS

Role plays are done in groups of four to six over eight hours or more. Participants simulate crisis center calls, one as the caller and one as the volunteer. Since the scenarios are not known beforehand, the volunteer gets a somewhat realistic idea of how it is to answer a call that could be about literally anything, and be ready.

Agora uses 20 or more scenarios, written up in enough detail to allow the caller to act and be able to talk at length about the problem. They are not reproduced here, but are things like:

- A 40-year-old calls about being bisexual and his failing marriage

- A 23-year-old was rejected from law school and does not know what to do next

Allow 10 minutes per call (shorter than reality). Allow timeouts to discuss what to do or deal with anxiety in the situation.

When the call is over, the one playing the caller and the one playing the listener self-evaluate, and then the lead people give additional feedback. Evaluation categories include:

- Did the listener match tone, build rapport, and make the space feel safe?

- Did they address feelings?

- Did they give enough time to explore before giving referrals or wrapping up?

Importantly, most feedback should be positive so the play-listener feels encouraged and can expand on what they do best. People listen in many ways, and the experience only needs to be effective for that particular pair of people; there is no generic objective rubric on which to judge performance.

How this helps

Role plays feel like a trial by fire, but without any actual risk of bad consequences. It can be like sitting for a test for a class that you did not take – everything coming at you is new and the answers cannot be rehearsed. All of the other training gives you knowledge in theory, but this is the practice that makes it real. The first chapter in the book gave examples of listening by reflecting, asking questions, and giving proof of understanding. The role play exercise is the main part of the curriculum that teaches someone how to do listening in that way.

First time role-players can be overconfident or underconfident. Often there is a mini-panic at pauses in the conversation: "I don't know what to say!" The lesson and transformation that ideally happens is internalizing how there is nothing that is perfect to say, and it has to come from inside, from what you hear in that moment. Thus it makes concrete the difference between pulling off a caring act versus actually caring, the difference between a clever idea from the listener's ego and a connected idea drawn from the caller, and the difference between leading and walking with. Some trainees have said the experience is humbling, or challenges the ego in a good way in a safe space.

In some scenarios, the caller's act connects to some reality in their life, and it becomes partly a real healing encounter, and not just a play. People cry and hug and need to support each other while debriefing the experiences. In this way what we do in training and for each other is what we do for the world.

Life force

PASSAGES ARE SPIRITUAL

Our culture is exceedingly bad at recognizing and even naming life transitions like the first loss, the break from linear life, retrenchment, psychic cycles, and the multidimensionality of older age. Robert Schumann wrote a beautiful simple piece, "First Loss" ("Erster Verlust"), which captures in music a feeling that is nearly impossible to express as richly in words. Our language and culture are a bit deficient in being able to talk about that common experience which is captured in that music.

One instance where some families bridge the realms of pain and growth and spirit is the first menstrual period. If looked at as a bad thing, it can just feel like a punishment dealt by some evil deity, or a new chore that one has to cope with and keep secret. But in some families it is celebrated as a sign of coming of age, which gives it a significance and even an honor. It brings the negatives into a common perspective with the larger reasons for it.

Other than a few examples like that, our culture tends to split "bad" things like loss and pain, from "good" things like achievements. In the psyche, though, these things are two sides of the same coin – fear goes with achievement; risk goes with reward. The Buddhist teaching that "life is suffering" does not mean that life is terrible; it means life is a path of psychic work. Schumann had to experience and cry over a first loss in order to express it in music.

Counselors can hold the hands of people going through these passages of development and help honor them. A psychic transition to the 2.0 version of yourself can feel like just plain depression and loss to a young adult, but we could choose to recognize and honor it as a passage and opportunity. While it is not helpful to assure people that there is definitely light at the end of the tunnel, it can be helpful to give people information about common journeys of other people, and have the confidence within ourselves that there is light at the end of the tunnel. The difference between assurance and confidence is subtle but important. We do not want to contradict the feelings people are having, or redirect them to think differently (such as the trite non-helpful reply that "it will all get better"), but we do want to shine a light on some openings and possibilities (such as "some people go through a period of dark confusion because they are remaking themselves – what would a new version of you be like?").

When crisis is very deep and becomes suicidal, the openness to the spiritual dimension also becomes ripe. The biggest change can be initiated when at the lowest point, like a springboard at the bottom of a fall.

"The secret of many a man's Success in the world resides in his insight into the moods of men and his tact in dealing with them."
— J. G. Holland

Anger is Like Drinking Poision and expecting The other Person to die.
— Buddha

FROM A PATH OF SUFFERING

Any authentic greatness that a person achieves – whether in the arts, in virtues, or in intellect – starts deep on the inside, and only the final result is seen on the outside.

The first couple minutes of the organ fugue in B minor by J.S. Bach, one of the greatest works in Western music, uses only seven notes, most of which are the same length in time. It is not about variation in volume, instrumentation, or rhythm, since organs do not allow for those kinds of variation. It is a quite simple structure, yet over centuries no one else has surpassed that level of expression with such a small set of tools.

Another example of simplicity is this poem by Rumi:

> A stone I died and rose again a plant;
>
> A plant I died and rose an animal;
>
> I died an animal and was born a man.
>
> Why should I fear? What have I lost by death?

I could not write this poem even though I can clearly see how simple the idea and words are. Why?

If a comedian says a few words and a million people laugh, how did he do it?

The external behavior of the composer, poet, or comedian can easily be copied but the much more significant internal process is unique and not reducible to elements. There is a long hidden path that came to the ability to express bigger things with fewer words or notes. The path has suffering and confusion, unique to the person, which no one can copy or teach. Not everyone achieves greatness like this but everyone is on a path – one that cannot be fully exposed, analyzed, or planned. Everyone needs to do work, struggle, and move in that private psychic way, regardless of outcomes. Molly says, "intervention is getting the person to the next moment in their life" – that is, in their particular life path.

SYSTEMS IGNORE THE INSIDE

Our modern systems of education and "behavioral health" are based mostly on the public part of human existence, as if there is no inner life or path. A person is always being measured on what they *show*. Great philosophers seem to all agree that discovering your uniqueness is more laudable than conformity, but actual policy promotes conformity and suppresses greatness. Our society is said to be "individualistic," yet we participate in systems that crush differences. As I write a plea to recognize that people are more than what we measure in schools, you the reader will say "of course" – it is obvious, yet we collectively fail to act on that knowledge. If we really believed it, we would treat children as gifts, gradually unfolding to fulfill their higher purpose, even when others do not see it.

Two empowering ideas that the modern institutions seem to ignore are the idea of the *path* and the idea of *burdens*. When I say "path," I'm referring to finding your way in life – finding the unique developmental path for you, or becoming what you were meant to be. Our institutions tend to define just one path that has been determined to be the best path of development for *everyone*, and they try to conform everyone to that path. Since we are all presumed to all be going down the same road, we can supposedly be measured: some are "ahead," some are "behind." But if you accept that you have unique inner gifts, then perhaps you have a unique path, and there is no ahead or behind.

Your particular burdens are those things that make your particular path difficult. We do not always know what a burden is; we feel resistance before we can identify the source. The source could be common and fairly obvious, or it might be unique and hard to name. You might feel unfairly burdened as if you are a target of a god's wrath. A past experience might slow you down to a crawl, but the same condition might not affect someone else. Regardless, we must carry our own burdens on our own paths. You cannot wish away burdens by coercing someone down a common path. Love can ease suffering, but it is not love to try to separate someone else's burdens or to prevent them from doing their work of carrying them.

FOUR SPIRIT QUESTIONS

The remainder of this chapter considers listening in a crisis on a more spiritual, life-long dimension that what has been covered so far, but it is still in line with the Agora listening model.

After hearing hundreds of people talk through their suicidal thoughts, I will tell you the main questions that have helped the most for illuminating the path – the ones that dig the deepest for a lot of people. These are questions I learned from people in crisis. These are:

- Who are you?

- Who hurt you?

- What do you feel?

- What is your quest?

Earth has a pushing life force; sky has a pulling life force.

When we are in a suicide crisis, it is not just because of one or a few isolated problems; the questions span from the distant past to the distant future and relate to the whole arc of life. We are all here to grow into our unique selves and fulfill a unique purpose. I visualize this arc as a person between earth and the sky. The earth is our past; energy flows from the ground into us, and the earth life force is a supporting springboard. The sky is our future and our options and ideals; its life force is pulling and opening.

When we are inclined to suicide, the life force is broken somewhere between earth and sky; there is no thread connecting the two poles of the life force. People in crisis may report a feeling of being trapped, drowning, and consumed by earth or water, or alternately they are floating with no ground and consumed by sky. Among other reasons, we can get this way because the robotic pressures of uniformity in our schools, families, and everywhere in the culture can crush the spirit and cut those threads. When the threads are weak and then we are suddenly victimized by a traumatic thing like rape, or if we lose a special person, there may not be enough resilience to reconnect the threads.

"Who are you" is a question that hurting people need to hear because it opens the non-judgmental topic of being an individual in the first place, and is a gateway question to the life force. Many people are living as a number on a scale – their grades, their income, or some rating of success – or they are living as a tool for someone else's boasting or manipulation. If I ask people if they are intro-verted, they might say they are *too* introverted and they have been working on being more social. But the question is not "what is wrong with you"; it is "who are you."

Knowing that you are introverted without saying it is a problem can be part of differentiating and honoring that the way of being is fine; also it starts to point to what you might be inclined to do with your life. Play the hand with the cards you were dealt since you cannot re-deal.

Some of the most commonly vilified human qualities are sensitivity, thrill seeking, and broad focusing. Sensitive children are so often told to get tougher and not to take things so hard. But these are the people who love universally and create harmony in the world, so it is a tragedy that our culture teaches sensitive people to hide.

Thrill-seeking children are told to stop, stop, stop – stop doing everything in your nature to do. "Be safe, don't be you." But we need people to take risks and push limits. It is true that a thrill seeker could die while parachuting or doing some other risky thing, but it is a bigger tragedy if they can never live as themselves in the first place.

Broad-focusing people are told to stay "on task" all the time and achieve pre-determined goals – other people's tasks and goals, not theirs. But to be truly alive, these people need to see connections between everything, and to create.

Other identifying questions can reveal logic versus feeling, independence versus family, creative versus receptive, and many other things. Just asking the question shifts away from right and wrong (a robotic question) towards being a unique human.

Along with being vilified, people who are a step away from the normal can get labels like borderline, autistic, or ADHD and be given medications or interventions which help in some ways but also may be geared towards making them less themselves. Some medications "work" by making people *less* in some way – less scattered, energetic or receptive – so they fit society better. My sense is that some medications risk interrupting the earth and sky energy flow as the cost of fitting in.

"Who hurt you" is a question that helps separate a person from what happened to them. It is important to name abusers and parents and others who applied pressure, and know that those things happened to us, but we did not do them. It is important to list both the big victimizing things like rape along with the ongoing patterns of minimizing that often are legal or even celebrated. For example, parents who "want the best" for their children and take it out on them by constant nagging and judging might be hurting them.

Some people in suicide crisis believe that they were themselves responsible for everything that happened to them. In the extreme it sounds like, "I had to be hit because I misbehaved." Anger is often absent, in the sense that the faculty for anger has been pried away from the person so that they would not have the power to retaliate. Part of getting out of that belief is asking the "who are you" question about the parents or partner. What kind of person are they? Knowing the qualities of the others (also without judgment) helps to see how they could do what they did, and that it wasn't the fault of the victim.

"How do you feel" is a question that our culture does not like to ask. We ask "how are you" but usually only want to hear one answer. It is important to ask and dig for nuanced descriptions because feelings are a gateway to needs; they illuminate what we need to do next. The more descriptive and accurate we can be, and the more a listener can understand feelings in detail, the more clear the needed actions become. While there are really only a few basic emotions (sadness, anger, fear, and a few others), they are made more complex in three main ways that I have seen. The first way is by being layered. Only the top feeling is easily accessible, while the ones underneath can be working without our knowing. For example, a person can be sad and not feel any anger but then after expressing the sadness and letting it be as big as it needs to be, it releases enough to see anger or some other feeling that was underneath.

A second complexity is how feelings are connected to thoughts and beliefs. Someone might say, "I feel like I want to die" or "I feel he might leave," and the way of saying that highlights the thinking more than the feeling. The first one could be feelings of despair, grief, or being overburdened, while the second one is a fear. Nudging the language towards more direct feeling words helps release the feelings more than is possible with the indirect language. It also opens connections to other things – for example, if we open up fear as part of our experience, we might realize we are afraid of more than what we originally were thinking about. The more trauma one is dealing with, the harder it is to access feelings.

A third complexity is in nuance. Some people want to die and others want to be dead, and others want to not be born. Those are very different. Likewise, the pain people experience is all different and just saying "pain" in not enough. It could be crushing, or lonely, or dull, or sharp, or sudden. One way to access the nuance of feelings when we don't find the words is to make a picture or story of it. For example: like a boat drifting in a wild current, or like a dry desert with no one for miles.

"What is your quest" is a question that I never ask in those words, but it is important to try to reconnect the thread to the sky force. Often a hurting person has to go way back to remember the future. "What did 10-year old Marcie want for her future" is a question I could ask 20-year old Marcie. Quests cannot be suggested or argued; they just arise from who we are, who hurt us, and what we feel. Contrary to popular advice, you cannot be anything you want; you can only be yourself. If a person is inclined to die, it almost always means she has no options; everything is blocked. It is important to center on the kind of quest that she actually has the power to do, and does not involve changing other people.

Working with people in crisis is great for so many reasons, and a big one for me is how they are willing to put everything on the table, and quickly explore dark places that more stable people are likely to wall off. Change has to be fast and often they are willing to change, so having these questions in mind can help them make a significant pivot in a single conversation.

Professionals

ENGINEERING AND ACCOUNTABILITY

In my childhood, airplanes crashed regularly. Now it has become more rare, though there are many more flights. The improved safety is largely due to changes in structure of organizations, not just because we know more or have better technology, or that people are more careful, or really anything about individual people. A similar thing has happened in a lot of fields – we have fewer building malfunctions such as electrical fires, improved traffic flow, and fewer accidents of nearly all kinds. In general we keep getting better at running complex systems.

With airplanes, the trend is to make accountability to safety a driving force in engineering procedures and company structures, so every proposed change gets vetted through different areas of expertise. A whole industry of failure analysis is strategically looped in so that myriad potential problems can be tested and corrected before anything is even built. Parts are cataloged in such a way that a defect found on one airplane can result in all parts from the same defective batch being replaced on all other airplanes, preventatively.

In a similar manner, if you apply for a building code variance or a zoning variance in a city, the request passes through various departments to check for problems. The fire inspector will examine the proposal for truck access, water capacity, egress, and materials selection. The environment manager will check for effluent, insulation, and related factors. The safety inspector will look for improper beam spans, the type of nails used, and so on. These people may be fairly unaware of what the other inspectors are looking for, focusing on their own area. And that is the point: there is no one person who can approve or deny an idea; it is a whole system of checks. Each person is more replaceable and their contribution is more transparent.

So far, I'm describing a good thing – a bureaucratization of things that used to be decided without as much hard evidence and sometimes decided by a single person. For lack of a better word, I am calling this "professionalizing" the industries. The word professional can indicate someone who is independently accountable and can make decisions without supervision. The bureaucratization process actually makes each individual person in the system *less* professional, but the system as a whole has a higher success rate. So when I say "professionalizing," I really mean the way the systems become more transparently accountable and more bureaucratic, and each person and relationship matters less.

You can see a downside of this trend in cashiers, call center staff, and other entry level workers. The cashier in a small business is able to make independent decisions, but now in big box stores they operate essentially as slaves to the computer. More and more aspects of life are becoming subject to the tentacles of big systems, and there is less room for creative solutions. It is a double-edged sword – we do not want people to do overly "creative" electric wiring, but it is also sad that cashier work can be so rigid, menial, and devoid of mind-expanding experiences.

ESL STORY

Now I will switch to the field of education, before getting back around to crisis centers. Schooling has become massively professionalized over my lifetime. Here is a story of my experiences teaching English as a Second Language (ESL) to adults in the 90s and again more recently. Back then, I volunteered to teach ESL with a fledgling nonprofit, and the experience was very inspiring for me and very effective for the students. I spent the majority of my time in that organization with students and they were speaking a lot of English; there was essentially no paperwork or management. I had complete leeway to find the ways that worked best for me and the learners, and I loved finding my way to do it and hear the learning happening rapidly.

Remembering how much fun that was, I attempted to get back into it 20 years later. I was unprepared for what I found – everything had changed. It was hard to even identify and reach an organization doing that kind of work, which confused me because I know that in Albuquerque the need is substantial. I tried organizing my own group with no luck, and finally found and went through a grant-funded class for learning how to teach ESL, which would ideally culminate with being assigned students. But the organization never did match me with anyone. I found a paid ESL teacher who agreed to accepting me as an assistant, but ultimately she would not ask me to work with them in any meaningful way. She was required to administer tests and follow a packaged curriculum. Like the big-box cashier I was spending all my time on being subservient to the system, going through trainings about goals and accountability and never actually teaching anything. The system had built up around a flow of money that did not previously exist, and the system was very self-protective. The paid teachers may have feared competition. The organizations had self-preservation in mind and were able to spend a lot of money and prove quantitative results, with little focus on real results – the ability to communicate effectively in English. What was once alive had become streamlined and mechanical.

Education and counseling are at root about relationships. Teaching is largely effective because of one-on-one unscripted relationships, regardless of which pedagogical or therapeutic system is being used. When you look back at elementary school teachers and think which ones you gained the most from, you would probably name the one that *cared* the most, whose love and support were most palpable. You probably would not name the one who used the most scientifically-proven-effective system of phonics.

VOLUNTEERS ARE MORE EFFECTIVE

Looking at the big picture here, we examined airplanes and the story of how professionalization of that industry has been stunningly positive, and we examined teaching and counseling, and how professionalization of that industry has been deadening. We may have developed a culture of professionalizing which started with engineering and has since spread to be mis-applied to everything else. There may be many other reasons, but the direction this is going with endeavors of human relations is very troubling.

It turns out that volunteer crisis centers may have better outcomes than professional ones. From a 2016 study[2]:

> Research since the 1960s has consistently found that lay volunteers are better at helping suicidal callers than professionals. Yet, professional degrees are increasingly becoming requirements for helpline workers. ... The volunteer centers more often conducted risk assessments, had more empathy, were more respectful of callers, and had significantly better call outcome ratings. ... We conclude from these results and previous research that there is no justification for requiring that suicide prevention helpline workers be mental health professionals. In fact, the evidence to date

2   Mishara, Brian & Daigle, Marc & Bardon, Cécile & Chagnon, François & Balan, Bogdan & Raymond, Sylvaine & Campbell, Julie. (2016). Comparison of the Effects of Telephone Suicide Prevention Help by Volunteers and Professional Paid Staff: Results from Studies in the USA and Quebec, Canada. Suicide & life-threatening behavior. 46. 10.1111/sltb.12238.

indicates that professionals may be less effective in providing telephone help to suicidal individuals when compared to trained lay volunteers.

While other research may have yielded other results, it is clear volunteers can be very effective. I believe the five main reasons for this are that volunteers spend more time with each person, they spend less time per week counseling, they are perceived more as equals with the person in crisis, they have less of an agenda, and they take more creative risks.

Time: Professional counseling costs more, so there is pressure to limit the time given to a caller. While this may look more efficient, that way of looking at efficiency is too narrow. Many times when I have spent an hour with someone and things remain murky, it is in the next 30 to 60 minutes with them when things really click together. If I had a time limit of one hour, the whole experience would have been mostly a waste, and that person would be back again the next day. Making a substantial discovery, even if it takes longer, is more efficient in the long run. This is similar to how fixing a car problem with a rigged up cheap solution involving duct tape (then having to do this multiple times because it does not last) can be more expensive in the end than fixing it right the first time. Spend the time and money up front!

Part-time: A larger set of volunteer counselors can work fewer hours (for less cost) than the equivalent number of professionals. It is important because the risk of burnout causes people to disengage from the experience. If it is only a few hours per week, you can put your whole self into it in a way is vulnerable and rewarding, and people in crisis really notice that level of engagement.

Equality: Listening compassionately really works, and especially when the perceived distance between the caller and listener is small. When we match tone and expressions with a caller and see them as an equal, avoiding advice-giving, judgment, or looking down on them in any way, they open up. A short-term relationship develops and both people can feel the bond of trust. Some professionals may have a hard time doing this, especially if they have a time limit.

Agenda: Professionals must be more accountable to their licenses and employers, and they have more liability on the line than volunteers do, generally speaking. Because of these factors, they may have more of an agenda, or a preconceived outcome for people in crisis. That agenda subtly or overtly puts pressure on the person to comply with advice. A volunteer at Agora, by contrast, discusses options but mainly gives space for the person in crisis to find their own way. After the call, we do not have to prove anything to anyone about how effective it was or if we did everything right.

Risk: Professionals will usually be risk-averse in the sense that they will stick to what has been proven and will be more concerned with their liability. So they are acting a bit more like airplane engineers. My experience has been that the more risks I take based on very slight rumblings of intuition, the better the result is. The more I do things by the book, the worse it comes out. The more I am genuinely me, the better. The more I am fitting the mold of a counselor, the worse. Like the rag-tag unstructured approach of my 90s ESL class, there can be bigger successes and bigger failures; less control and accountability means there will be more variation in relationships and outcomes.

This next point could sound controversial: *In crisis counseling, failures do not kill people; the worst outcome is neutral.* But in engineering, failures do kill people. Thus the approach to professionalization has to be different between those two endeavors. This is counter-intuitive to some because it seems like saying the wrong thing to someone who is about to suicide is such a high risk, and one has to be extra-careful when they are at the edge. But it is the opposite: the counselor needs to take more risks, bend the rules, grasp at straws, and try to access unexplainable intuition in these cases. The same old advice is guaranteed to never work, so the only thing that might work is stretching the limits. The person at that level of crisis has probably already heard all the "correct" interventions and one more ineffective conversation will not by itself push them closer to dying. The counselor's power to accidentally "make them pull the trigger" is tiny compared to all the other influences in life that brought them to that point.

...EVEN IN EXTREME CASES

As the reader you might be thinking that people with higher levels of crisis, or more disabling trauma, or complex mental health conditions might need a more professional service, while those with a more relatable level of trouble can be helped by volunteers. I have not found this to be true. Indeed I have had conversations where I suggested a therapist, but the person answered they had been in and out of hospitals for a decade and seen dozens of professionals. Sometimes they say that none of it helped, or that it was all just piling on more trauma layers. In those cases where there seem to be no more sources of help, if any technique can help, that technique will be nonjudgmental compassionate listening, which a non-professional can do.

The system of psychiatrists and hospitals is not even set up to handle extremes very well, from what I hear from ex-patients. Extreme patients may be combative or "treatment resistant" in various other ways so the treatment can get adversarial. The lack of autonomy, up to and including incarceration and 24-hour monitoring can be highly traumatizing (even if it is necessary) and sets up conditions where little real healing can occur. The system cannot know what to do with someone who has an extreme history, such as being sold as a sex slave to a priest, then developing multiple personalities and a drug addiction. These things do happen, and they are beyond the ability of the rest of us or the system as a whole to know what to do with. People in that state of suffering are very lonely in their quest to get help: the system essentially shrugs helplessly and has no answer.

I know someone who regularly calls crisis lines, and he says Agora is the best. People calling tell us that regularly as well during the calls. His level of traumatic experiences is extreme. He gets enraged calling professional-staffed lines because he says they do not really listen and they jump to giving advice, but that advice is not informed by the unimaginable years of torture he went through. But at Agora, a young college student who has never even heard of such atrocities can still listen. He says (paraphrased), "As long as they are willing to listen and help me feel through whatever I am feeling, that is worth it. They don't have to know how to fix anything."

OTHERING

When white Americans say, "This is our country!" it is a subtle and powerful form of racism because the speaker and listener alike know what "our" means, without spelling it out. It is implying that America belongs to people like "us," not like "them." Depending on context, "them" could mean, for example, people from Mexico or some other group that is not like the speaker in ethnicity, language, or culture. But at the same time, if pressed, the speaker can weasel out of it by saying they meant something else, and claim that of course they are not racist. The power of political dog-whistling in this manner comes from the semi-unconscious nature of the language used, allowing people to sidestep self-scrutiny. In the extreme, white nationalist rallies in recent years have featured flags, anthems, calls for "freedom," chants of "taking back" something unnamed, and similar non-specific symbology. This process of creating a deep feeling of "us" separate from "them" is known as othering, and it is an essential part of racism.

Othering also happens in less extreme ways and it can be hard to see because it is not spelled out and does not necessarily have national ramifications like the example above. An office might have a team composed of mostly men and one woman, and the woman might think that everyone is equal for some time. But then one of the men says something like, "We think you should lead the year-end review."

The woman is not excluded, but "we" was used to indicate the group holding soft power in that setting, without being explicit. Perhaps the guys went out after work and talked when she was not there. The person being othered can easily feel it while the others may insist they never made any such distinction.

In the helping arenas of counseling and social services, it is easy to slip into othering no matter how much we try not to. The model is usually set up as professional people providing services to clients, so the very structure of being paid, reporting on outcomes, and making judgments about progress creates the line between us (providers) and them (clients). In order for the organization to function, each person has to be in one of the two roles.

So why is this a problem in this context? Othering takes away autonomy in the sense that it takes away the voice of the othered; they are not being heard and they are not in on the main decisions of a group, or they are not even in on the decisions made about themselves. For someone accessing help with a crisis, they are most likely experiencing reduced autonomy – a cornerstone reason why people get into a deep crisis in the first place. So when accessing a professional system of help that has an us/them model of othering built into it, they can feel even further reduced autonomy and even more of a crisis.

When the response is to take someone against their will to a locked hospital situation, it can feel essentially like holding the cage low in the water with only a tiny bit of air. Most of us can easily imagine how that could be a trauma-inducing experience, but even lesser forms of othering can trigger traumas.

PROFESSIONAL MODEL

As opposed to the circles model used at Agora, a professional model might look more like this:

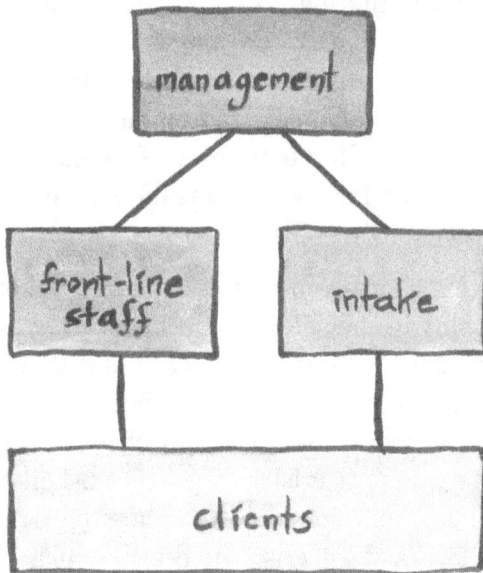

The professional model inherently creates an us/them separation, while the circles organizational model tends to erase that distinction.

I have been fortunate to be able to work in Agora's model, but there have been jarring reminders that other models exist. The National Suicide Prevention Lifeline (NSPL), a much larger operation that seems to operate in a more professionalized way, sometimes gives us evaluations.

Agora evaluations are all about our collective education and growth; they are participatory, supportive, and give volunteers the benefit of the doubt. By contrast, the NSPL evaluations are essentially lists of mistakes. The message that goes with that kind of evaluation is: "take no risks; be replaceable."

For background, many of the crisis lines started as volunteer in the 1970s, and later became more professionalized. Some have been assumed by state control and some have become for-profit. Agora is one of the only volunteer centers left that serves the general public.

The new 988 funding requirements are paving the way to the end of crisis volunteering. Money could dry up for Agora, as funders may not understand why volunteer organizations still need funding, and they may not understand the benefits of a model like Agora in the way this book describes.

A larger corporate call center doing this work has even lobbied the legislature *against funding Agora,* citing that they only hire degreed clinicians, and that Agora is not "real help." When successful, this siphons a lot of money out of what could be a much more efficient use of it.

MANDATED REPORTING AND AUTONOMY

One of the differences between Agora and many other options that a person can reach out to is that Agora volunteers are not "mandated reporters." That term refers to people who are legally required to report harm or threats that they hear, even if they hear those things in confidential settings. For example, a teacher is (usually) legally required to report evidence of abuse that they might discover from a child, and a therapist must report a client's plans for violence.

The advantages to mandated reporting are fairly obvious: we need to be able to avert crimes and suicides, and we do not want teachers and others to be off the hook when they knew information that could have helped avert a crime.

But consider also the advantages of true confidentiality. Knowing that no one will repeat my secrets allows me to share the secrets, which unburdens me of them: this is part of the healing process. People need a place to talk about taboo things, maybe abuse from parents, but they do not want to disrupt their lives quite yet – they just first need to talk. Consider men who have the compulsion of pedophilia, and even if they do not want to hurt others, they live with a compulsion of constant intrusive thoughts and virtually everyone would be horrified to hear about it. So one of the main paths to healing is blocked from them – expressing the pain. When there is a support group available to them which guarantees confidentiality, that opens up a healing avenue, and that could ultimately avert crimes.

One can draw the line in many places. When professional liability is involved, people tend to err on the side of caution. For example, a teacher may report a scar on a child's arm that was most likely caused by something innocuous like a game of tag – but they might be afraid of their own liability if it turned out to be an unsafe home. At Agora we err more on the side of confidentiality. People can talk about thoughts, including thoughts of violence or suicide or pedophilia, without being reported. Of all the calls received, only a tiny fraction result in help being sent, because we are able to reduce risks most of the time through listening. Of the times help is called, it is mostly for a suicide in progress, and only once in a blue moon is there a need to report planned violence. So the philosophy there is that thoughts, and even starting to form plans, are safe to talk about, but dangerous actions that are actually in progress will be escalated.

Before reading my thoughts below, consider where you would draw the line. Should minors be handled differently than adults? At what age? What about someone who is planning a school shooting?

Hopefully you stopped to consider before reading on. My answer to this dilemma after a lot of pondering is that there needs to be a place where people can talk about anything anonymously, no matter how horrific it is. Yes, that means a counselor would be burdened with some very heavy information. A counselor could even read about a school shooting that they knew might happen because they had talked with the shooter the day before, and have to live with the guilt of not preventing it. On the other hand, it could also happen that a potential shooter decides not to follow through after being able to talk about it confidentially. Remember that virtually no one's first choice is a mass shooting; that is something they only get to after many other things have failed. They wanted to be accepted, heard, and included; violence happens after they have given up on what they really needed. At the end of the book, I will list some more specific ideas.

As a final note on this, consider how breaking confidentiality is a form of denying autonomy. Someone may have thought their secrets were safe but then come to find out they have been reported. Since autonomy is a basic need that is so closely tied to suicide, being a trustworthy and honest listener when it comes to keeping secrets allows people to keep their autonomy intact, and thus saves lives.

Even where we do not allow complete confidentiality for minors, we need to change how we do the reporting. If a school counselor says, "well, I notified the parents, so my job is done!" then they have just escalated a situation: the parents might not know what to do, trust is broken between the teen and their circle of adults, and conflict could be provoked in the family. Instead it has to be reported and escalated in a transparent way, involving the minor, and bringing in the resources needed to solve the problem.

LIMITS OF PSYCHOLOGY

Psychology as practiced today does not cover the full breadth of healing. It includes a lot of things, like talk therapy of many forms, medicine, and brain disease, but people can heal in other ways. Most notably these other paths are religious healing through prayer and ritual, activism to change the system that is the source of a problem, body-focused approaches like massage or sports, and nontraditional options like magnets, essential oils, and psychedelics.

Regardless of what you believe about each of these approaches, it is clear that psychology has been quite narrowly focused on individuals being diagnosed and then guided using techniques that are supposedly proven. While there are branches such as social psychology and occupational therapy, which are informed by family systems and the biopsychosocial comprehensive model, the dominant pattern of the field is closer to the sequence: "individual is broken; diagnose; fix." These are not necessarily critiques of psychology, but rather a critique of the belief that the system of professionalized psychology is the only way or the best way to ease crisis or suffering.

I heard of a natural disaster in South Africa to which the US sent doctors, including psychologists, to help in the aftermath. The culture clash yielded poor therapy results because the concept of healing there was so different than in the US. Leaders there felt the affected people would be better served by high energy and physically close things like dances rather than talk therapy where everyone is separated. Whether the story is accurate or not, it highlights how the US culture tends towards individualistic, rational solutions and can overlook community actions and non-rational mind-body solutions.

At the extreme, the system can focus only on wellness of the individual regardless of the brokenness of their environment. A shy student in a school of 4,000 who is bullied and excluded may be treated for her depression, as if she is expected to be able to be happy in those circumstances. A sick system should make people angry enough to change it, not just deal with their depression or "anger issues" as if they can be corrected completely in isolation.

In a more general way, the spiritual arc of life, which could be rich with discovery, is sometimes de-emphasized when someone is "sick" because of a false assumption that you have to be "OK" on a basic psychiatric level first before seeking greater enlightenment. But the life force that ultimately makes us OK is a spirit that is greater than us. The more broken someone feels, the more they need all these bigger things of the spirit; learning to just cope and becoming stable cannot be the prerequisites because stability by itself does not really give us anything substantial to live for.

The more professional the systems of crisis support get, the more they will be boxed within these limitations.

Social justice

A PARALLEL TO PROFESSIONALIZATION

Like professionalization, the social justice movement is another trend that is a double-edged sword, both informing and threatening the sphere of crisis response.

I will use the acronym SJ for social justice when I am referring to the somewhat codified, rule-based, or ideological form of the movement that is associated with the political polarization going on in these times. It is much narrower than justice as a general concept, and it is what conservatives deride as "wokeness" because of the specificity of its rules. While basically everyone is in favor of justice in the generic sense, SJ as I am using the term here is more particular and is politically contested.

Some of the positives of SJ include narratives informed by topics such as trauma, systemic marginalization, and the minutiae of white supremacy. Youth culture increasingly embraces the language of trauma and triggers, and the connection between that and systematic oppression. These are concepts that would have been like a foreign language a generation or two ago. Many, including liberal white people, are now more aware of their internalized white supremacy, and how it gets expressed in myriad subtle patterns that favor white males, such as tone policing and standards of appearance.

Some of the negatives of SJ include cancel culture, rigidity, and a rejection of compassionate listening. Ironically the hierarchical ranking and systems of marginalization in the wider culture may be mirrored within the ranks of those activists who are fighting against those problems. The rest of this chapter will get into some of these ideas in more detail.

LISTENING ACROSS THE AISLE

Agora teaches a kind of compassion that has been noticeably on the wane since the US fell toward extreme polarization in the 2010s.

That compassion is listening to people you do not agree with. Suppose you, as the volunteer, are gay and are talking to someone who claims "the gays" are responsible for all problems; you still have to listen to them. Actually it is more like listening through the words, beyond it to other things that are a layer down. Even if they ask what you think should be done to "eliminate the gays," you still must reflect on the question with them without exploding, and use it to discover the pain and other feelings under it. This is what therapists, and the helping professions in general, are trained to do – bite their tongues and avoid being judgmental even if the client is expressing hate.

Outside of Agora, on college campuses, the spreading social justice (SJ) ideology is composed of numerous rules about what words are the correct ones to refer to groups of people, which identities can be claimed by whom, and who is allowed to talk about certain things. While most of these ideas originated in actual struggles against oppression and with formalization from academics in critical theory and sociology, it is notable how nearly no critical thought or dialectic methods remain after the ideas moved out of academia to social media interactions. There, the street version of social justice is more of a rule-based ideology than a type of inquiry. It seems to involve lashing out and being judgmental as a core principle.

Meanwhile, another huge chunk of conservative America has shifted to the right.

Volunteers in recent years may have had an increasing struggle when balancing the Agora way of expressing compassion with the SJ ideology of how to be a good person. Lots of people have to code-shift to adapt to different environments, where the communication patterns are different – for example, family, church, and school. A code-shift suggests a slight change in language and expressed attitude around different people, but now it is a bigger leap, not a slight shift. Agora remains fairly centrist in the map of American side-taking, thus it gets farther from both the extreme left and the extreme right. Is there a breaking point beyond which left-leaning volunteers cannot shift into Agora mode?

SJ-HEALTH CONNECTION

Let us pause a moment on the idea that trauma and justice are connected at all. As I speculated earlier in the Trauma chapter, the better understood the connection is in society, the more this understanding exposes systemic oppression and would lead to more equality. Thus there is incentive for elites to exert political pressure to keep these domains separate. Healing individuals and healing the system must be interconnected for the success of either, and separating the two domains is a way to prevent either one from succeeding. Trauma, when looked at only from the mental health domain, raises questions like: "how can we help this person?" – the problem and solution being seen as within each individual. But when looked at from an SJ perspective, the questions become more about who is right or wrong, who is privileged and who is voiceless, and who owes whom. So on the one side, the individual is broken, and on the other side, the system is broken.

Even from the SJ perspective there can be pressure to keep these domains separate. In the developmental disability world for example, there is a contingent of people who stress that "nothing is wrong" with disabled people, and any effort to "heal" them is misguided. In my work in that context, I have gotten push-back for even talking about growth at all. People have remarked that those with disabilities do not need to change. To me, that falsely conflates healing or growth with reprogramming or normalizing. There is a giant industry dedicated to normalizing people with developmental disabilities, and it is oppressive because it is about changing that population to fit the needs of others; it is not about what the population needs. But everyone still deserves to heal and change. To be protected from challenging growth opportunities in the name of justice is a dangerous limiting factor in one's life path.

IDEOLOGY VS CRITICAL THINKING

A turning point in my thinking about where I stand on the political spectrum came when I was trying to communicate in a Facebook group focused on racial justice. A cornerstone topic in those circles is the guilt felt by white people for the violence and colonialism practiced by their ancestors, and which is continuing today. Depending on how radical the group declares itself, it may not only make the claim that white people *feel* guilty, but that they *are* guilty and have unpaid debts to people of color as a population. In this group, they went even further and said that all white people are morally and legally culpable for those crimes by virtue of ancestry. The group had an ideological purity and seemed to speak as one voice, frequently batting down any dissent or questioning. I insisted that their position was essentially "guilt by association" which is an abhorrent and morally primitive concept which has been used to justify many injustices including slavery. Their comeback was that I was experiencing white fragility and was rationalizing my privileges as a way to stonewall progress. I was just labeled wrong, period, no discussion. I left that particular group and realized from an accumulation of such experiences that I was not as "radical" as these loud voices in the SJ movement.

When we are wrapped up in a way of thinking, it can be very hard to distinguish ideology from critical thinking. Ideology is marked by definite answers without discussion, and pressure for everyone to believe alike. Critical thinking is marked by questions without full answers, and a divergence of conclusions. Joining an ideology is alluring: I have wanted to be right, be part of something, and be on the right side of history, and those cravings have made me more ideologically unbending at times. But recently it felt liberating to give up on the idea of being a progressive in that way.

There is always a risk of false dialog between dominant and marginalized people. A true dialog would have people on equal footing where one side does not control the culture and rules of engagement. But in a world where white men often feel like the natural born arbiters of everything, they tend to only engage with others when they are the majority in the room and only if it all feels "nice and respectful" to them. These conditions impede actual communication and negotiation: there cannot be substantial change until the dominant people feel uncomfortable and lose their power to control the dialog. No one gives up dominance because someone asked nicely.

For those reasons, I think the SJ movement is wary of the idea of compassionate listening. It feels like giving up the battle by being too nice and compromising. I felt that my opinions on guilt by association were not being listened to at all, and that I was escalating a sense of conflict by merely expressing my thoughts. It could feel like a false dialog for them to engage with me if it felt like I was trying to argue against change as a rationalization for maintaining my privileged position in society as a white person.

While there are coherent reasons for being wary, when taken to the ideological extreme, it leads to squashing dissent and ending dialog. This closes the door to genuine internal growth. Purity tests for belonging to a group or movement cause a system of ranked inequality within the groups, as competition to control the message pushes down everyone less powerful. What could have been a movement that is informed by the need for equality and for healing can be so toxic that it does neither.

And the biggest irony is that the SJ movement has a tendency to throw out longstanding principles of justice that underpin our current legal protections. One of these is the principle of no guilt by association, as discussed above. Another is the principle of presumption of innocence. In the actual legal system, in order for punishment to occur, the prosecution has to prove that a crime was committed, citing the rule that was violated. Each of us has an assumed contract with society that requires us to know the laws. Depending on the crime and the specific situation, establishing intent may be necessary. There is no legal protection for people feeling hurt or insulted, and as long as what we are doing has not been established as a rule violation, we are free to do it no matter how others feel about it. But in the SJ world, a court of public opinion can label people as violators and cancel them regardless of intent and regardless of their knowledge of the "rule" in question. There can be no contract with society because the rules may be unwritten and capricious. So the form of "justice" within the SJ movement can be barbaric.

TRIGGERS AND HEALING

As I wrote earlier in the book, having one's trauma trig-gered can bring it into light and help understand and heal it, as long as that triggering is really just bringing up a memory and not a re-traumatization.

The SJ culture, though, does not seem to be on board with this idea. A new idea is that triggering someone else inad-vertently is a wrong – a wrong that makes the triggerer guilty. People feel the need to put trigger warnings on writing, and that not doing so is a form of harm. Professors have been blamed for discussing violence or other trig-gering topics as if they were actually being violent. People self-censor in order to avoid being canceled by peers.

Molly says she sees that teens now have triggers they are more aware of, and they consider triggering to be a wrong against them. More people in trainings are leaving the room, turning away, or quitting due to being triggered. She muses that teens do not have as much resiliency as before. For example, just the word "angry" can be triggering. This generation is more likely to expect the same consideration for feeling sad as for actual PTSD.

In fact, Molly tries to trigger people purposefully. In order to hear what people need to talk about in a crisis, we have to work on our own triggers, not just expect the world to collectively shield us from any bad feeling. Without that work, we cannot really hear each other's deepest truths.

Molly's approach appears to be increasingly contested though.

CLAIMING LABELS

In SJ ideology, people claim labels to be an authentic member of a marginalized group or some other identity group. A blog post might identify the author as being "mixed race, multiply disabled, and queer." These words are listed as if they are credentials, and to some extent it does make sense that a queer person would be more qualified to talk about queer issues. But it goes beyond identification: these words are claims which can be disputed – and often are. In economics, a market system exists when the supply of a commodity is limited, and similarly in the SJ space, labels are commodities that are limited by disputing their authenticity. Some on-line fighting in the SJ world questions whether some foe is "really" mixed race, queer, etc. with the understanding that stripping them of the label takes away their platform and power. It is popular these days to let people know that one is part native American, that being a label with high social value. Senator Elizabeth Warren did this and then backpedaled after an SJ storm erupted in response. The question at the heart of that battle is whether she was justified in claiming the label, or if it was just grabbing at a token based on a tiny percent of native ancestry. Like a pound of rolled oats, or any other commodity, the supply has to be limited in order to have value. Something either is, or is not, a pound of rolled oats – it is not a question of perspective. And likewise in an ideologically pure framework, a label such as being part native has to be definite and limited. Ideologies breed sloppy thinking in this way, since in reality, one's ethnic characteristics are always a matter of perspective and of degree.

Along with this, there has been a dizzying multiplication of labels for gender and sexuality in the last decade. I recently met someone in her 20s, and in getting to know each other, she offered that she was a pan-sexual demi-girl. Since I am a generation older, this descriptor gave me no information, and I did not have a set of labels for myself to offer in response.

Labels can also include diagnoses, any minority status, or emotional conditions like being a survivor or a child of narcissistic parents.

LOUDNESS: "I'M NOT WORRIED ABOUT HIM; HE'S SCREAMING"

Someone once told me they were not really a rape survivor because that word is limited to people who said "no"; in her case she failed to verbalize that, so in her mind she is not allowed to "own" that label. Someone else wondered out loud to me if they should own a diagnostic label when they did not have the condition as acutely as someone else. These are examples of people being careful not to appropriate a label that they may not be allowed to have. Being "good" is staying invisible.

There is a continuum from loud, often competitive people with many social media followers who claim, control, and arbitrate the labels, down to people who meekly knock on the door of the SJ hierarchy inquiring about admittance. This exposes the system of oppression built into the SJ movement itself: that the most voiceless among us do not get to own our labels. When the narrative of oppression is controlled by people who are only slightly oppressed, those further down the ladder are erased. As someone who has felt relatively voiceless and never a part of any activist movement, I have asked myself, "why are people so darn entitled to their voices?" At times I have heard people give impassioned speeches at a podium, then gone home, and much later realized I experience the same or more of the marginalization they were talking about, yet I am never the one at the podium. And there are so many more voiceless than me, whom we may never hear from.

The following story shows a parallel of the loud/quiet distinction: I was at the scene of a car accident. A single person in one of the cars was unhurt, but the the other car with a couple in it had crunched and deployed the air bag. The man was running around yelling in pain, having gotten out of the crashed car. The woman was sitting quietly in the car. As an untrained observer, it felt like she was probably not hurt and that the man needed attention. But the EMT urgently asked me to help with the woman, and said, "I'm not worried about him: he's screaming." With the EMT's training, it was obvious that the man did not have a spinal injury or a punctured lung, while the woman's quietness signaled that she might have something like those serious injuries.

We all need to be like that EMT. We need to pay more attention to what people actually are going through, not pay more attention to the people who are more successful at using their voice to draw attention to their pain.

STAYING IN YOUR LANE

One dictum of SJ is "stay in your lane," which means to speak from your own experience. It may be directed at people of relative privilege, such as white people trying to opine about or solve problems of non-white people as a group. To me, this is helpful advice up to a point: It is helpful to establish boundaries that allow people with similar experiences to solve in-group issues and communicate openly without the intrusion of false allies, saviors, or detractors who are not part of that group. It also speaks to how sometimes a person needs a friend or therapist who is in their same category – such as a woman, person of color, or the same religion – because you can start with shared knowledge and values, allowing the conversation to leap ahead versus when talking to someone not in the category.

Lately, in some circles, this has been taken to an ideologically extreme place, where it connects to claiming labels, and where only those deemed to deserve the labels can occupy the "lane." People will even say: "you are not allowed to have an opinion on this." The problem is that stripes on a highway are high-contrast markers that divide up the lanes unambiguously, but there are no such strict lines in the human population. Attempts to enforce who is in which lane can leave a lot of people out of any lane.

In medicine, some people look for their own kind – such as women seeking a female obstetrician. It is uncomfortable for some to trust someone who is not a woman on matters of pregnancy, either because of the very personal nature of it, or the belief that a male doctor could not fully understand. On the other hand, if you need an appendectomy, you would not be likely to limit yourself to surgeons who have themselves had that surgery. For most medical help, we trust that the doctor can do it because of their training, not because they have experienced the same problem. In general, experts should be equally competent despite their personal experiences.

When it comes to crisis counseling, listening across a divide of experience is an issue, but it is a chasm that can be crossed. For example, I have a much easier time understanding what women who are prone to depression are going through than what men who are prone to anger are going through, because of having much more overlapping life experiences with the former group. But since we are not experts in anything, we need to listen to whatever experience someone is having, no matter how different, without assuming that it is anything like our own experiences. Even if a crisis counselor does happen to be an expert in something, it is important to set that aside because listening is not an exercise in showing expertise. I have bridged a lot of chasms by listening, so with experience, everyone feels a bit closer. For example, I did not know about some of the common experiences of American born daughters of Indian parents, but I have heard, and I now snap to understanding quicker when talking to someone with those experiences. I had the same initial distance from people with eating disorders, thrill-seeking types, and veterans, all of which feel closer now.

Some have proposed ways to match identities with callers so that everyone can stay in their lane – men only talking to male callers, and so on. Agora will not do this, for both practical and philosophical reasons. The practical reason is we do not have a room full of idle people of all types who can be called on to hand off a call, and the disturbance of doing a hand-off would not be helpful. The philosophical reason is that we are all different anyway, even if we appear to be in the same category in SJ terms, and so we always have to bridge a distance with people, and that is part of the growth process for both parties. Being in a certain category is not a qualification.

THE THREAT TO AGORA

Here is a quick anthropology lesson that will be used to illustrate an analogous point later: In different cultures, people have an agreed distance apart that feels normal – some cultures having a much wider separation than others. A Ugandan talking with an Argentinian may experience constant adjustment as the Ugandan backs up to be comfortable, thinking the Argentinian is being invasive; at the same time the Argentinian may keep advancing, thinking that the Ugandan is rude for being so remote. Neither one is being rude; they are just encultured differently.

Last year at Agora, a violation of personal space boundaries occurred in the office. I will skip the details because I do not want to identify anyone. It was a conflict that was seen differently by the two sides, perhaps a bit like the cultural differences between countries as described above. The person named as the violator of personal space did not see it as a violation. The group of people who felt violated escalated it to the level of a social justice issue, namely an act of micro-aggression or even full-out oppression. They adopted a posture of strength in numbers rather than an approach of listening.

We are trained to deal with conflicts with callers and with each other in the Agora way, which is listening and not jumping to judgment or conclusions. Callers may have distasteful opinions but we still give them space to talk. In this incident, the SJ ideology overtook the Agora way. My sense is that, historically, people were able to attend rallies and demand social change wearing an activist hat, and also engage in counseling wearing the Agora hat, and it was possible for people to have multiple sides to their lives at the same time without issue. They could compartmentalize. But lately, SJ has spread and colonized more areas in life in a way that demands total obedience, so now some people are seeing Agora, and the classroom, and sports, and everything as inside the SJ domain.

Of course injustices can occur anywhere, and the argument here is not that certain spaces should be exempt from trying to achieve the ideals of justice and equality. In fact, when any space is walled off in that way and kept out of sight, hurts and crimes can flourish in secrecy, such as what has happened in Catholic and other churches. So we absolutely should be seeking justice everywhere.

Where I think SJ thinking is a threat to a communication and growth type of space like Agora is in the means and tactics. There is a difference between actual justice and the political tactics used to achieve justice. It can make sense to use agitation, displays of strength, coordinated disobedience, and other destabilizing tactics in the political sphere to drum up the anger needed to clean out corruption. Those techniques are used when simpler methods have not worked. But it is damaging to jump to those techniques immediately, because they destroy relationships. Compassionate listening builds unity and promotes healing, and that should always be the first step. Fighting may prove a point, but at the expense of the whole organization.

Therefore, there is still a need to compartmentalize and be part of the SJ culture where it is appropriate, but resist it in places like Agora.

The threat of SJ ideology is similar to the threat of professionalism as discussed in the last chapter. Both have a tendency to spread tentacles and take over more areas of life. Both normalize ways of being and ways of communicating, making things scripted instead of alive.

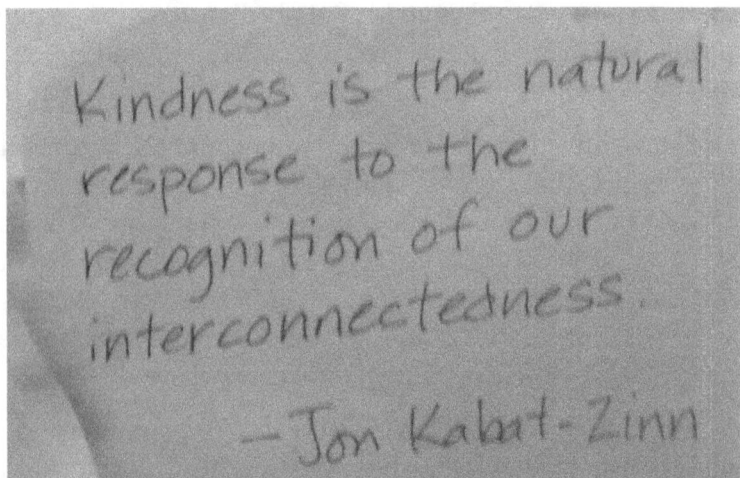

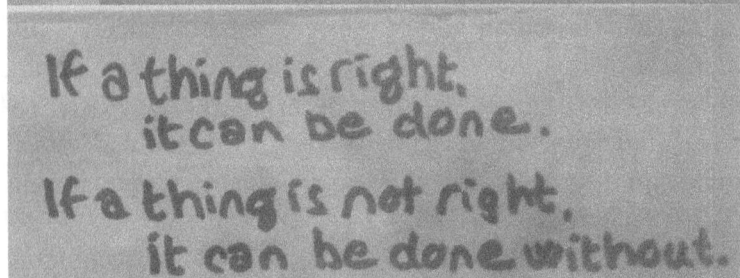

Kindness is the natural response to the recognition of our interconnectedness.

— Jon Kabat-Zinn

If a thing is right, it can be done.
If a thing is not right, it can be done without.

IDENTITY AND BIAS

An important thing I absorbed from Michelle and Barack Obama is the unwavering philosophy that we are all one people, not competing groups of races or classes. Of course they are aware that race and class conflict are central in American history and current politics, but their language showed that those are just problems and not the under-lying truth. When any issue involving race or any kind of group identity came up in the era of his presidency, many politicians and observers would characterize it as a group conflict, and use the words "we" and "they" in a way that identifies where the speaker stands. The Obamas would invariably use "we" to mean all of us, and identify victims of discrimination as individuals rather than as a bloc.

Going into this a little more, there are three distinct ways to think about and talk about discrimination, which I am calling *dismissing, fighting, and unifying*.

The *dismissing* way is usually heard from those who are privilege-blind and see the world in terms of the categories. An example is someone who says: "I don't mind if gay people live in my neighborhood – I'm not prejudiced or anything, but I just don't want them indoctrinating our kids in school!" Even if they see themselves as accepting, they are still showing that being straight is normal or correct, that being gay is an aberration, and that children should be taught only about those normal/correct families. Many children's books depict straight people, but they do not see those materials as "indoctrination" – even if they are saying either way of being is fine with them. Another example is someone I heard interviewed recently who said: "I don't mind if there are black people in our county, but they just need to respect our laws." The unspoken assumptions in that sentence are louder than the words; the we/they thinking is so strong that it is hard to believe the speaker really "doesn't mind."

The *fighting* way is heard more in SJ circles and goes along with claiming a group identity, staying in one's lane, and working on behalf of a specific group. Those not in the group should (according to the ideology) declare allegiance to it while being careful to identify oneself as not in the group. Someone might say, "I'm fighting for the rights of my LGBTQ brothers and sisters!"

The *unifying* way of the Obamas sounds more like, "If any one of us is victimized or discriminated against on the basis of their sexual orientation, we need to protect that person." In this worldview, "we" is everyone and the existence of socially constructed factions is minimized.

The dismissing and fighting ways are opposing camps, but they are also two sides of the same coin. One way labels groups as oppressors versus oppressed; the other labels groups as normal versus different; but they both see upper and lower tiers of society and see themselves as on one of the two sides. Both have a tendency to blame the other side for the problems. That fight plays out in some crude ways, trying to determine who is racist, sexist, homophobic, and so on.

The unifying way, by contrast, has the potential for looking for causes of discrimination in you, and in me, and in all of us. In that worldview, we do not need to declare allegiance to "them" (any marginalized group) because our struggle is broader: to protect *ourselves* – all of us.

Molly introduces these topics by talking about "bias" –
specifically our own biases, without going into the territory
of determining the bias of anyone else, or even bringing up
any of the -ism words.

A training that uses the language of examining all of our
biases can feel more palatable to those in relative privilege,
like white males, than a training that assigns group identity
labels and blame. The latter is likely to provoke defensive
responses. From an SJ perspective, though, the former
approach may feel like coddling, and even pretending that
there is equal bias on all sides, which ignores that there are
definite systemic strata of privilege. To me, both sides are
true – that anyone can have biases, but at the same time,
those with privilege accrue more power to weaponize their
bias.

I worked in a large financial company once whose lowest
tier of employees was majority black females, while
management was cornered by white males. We had to go
through bias training of the sort that is palatable and
presented in such a way as to avoid provoking defensive-
ness. A couple things about this were surprising. One is
how some very powerful messages about equality made
their way into these inner passageways of capitalism,
where I expected a very pro-forma type of training. They
had hired people who understood the subject very well and
gave real world examples – such as how an English accent
spoken natively in India can be falsely labeled as wrong by
Americans and result in a power differential. But the other
surprising thing is how there was a wall in the corporate
culture dividing the topics in the training from what you
were actually allowed to talk about. If someone failed to
pick up on those unwritten taboos about office talk, and

mentioned to their coworkers how ironic it is that white management is pushing this training on employees that were mostly minorities, or if they mentioned a specific person whom they thought was unfairly treated due to race, color, or other bias, then that person would be swiftly disciplined or fired. The ultimate message from the training is: "just never mention anything about this topic to keep your job."

Bringing this back to Agora, what is the best way to talk about -isms and bias? I feel that Molly has expertly threaded the needle here. In Agora training, we talk about our own bias, but we also expose relative privilege. There is no prohibition of office talk like in the financial company. But there is also not a stress on assigning guilt as in the SJ movement. Even without the dimension of guilt, the trainings can be uncomfortable, which is essential to recognize the need for internal change. Ultimately, like everything else Molly does, it is presented to be educational, even transformative, and balances the discomfort with safety, so it is a true learning environment.

The *way* we talk about bias also reflects *why* we need to talk about it. The direct reason at Agora is because we need to be able to bridge language, cultural, and other differences with callers. The reason is not to wake up to the need for a revolution, or to fight for (or against) equality. But ironically, Agora *is* changing the world by working on building those bridges. You do not have to be a crisis counselor to have the need to span the distance to people who seem different. Being grounded in this reason for having a conversation about racism and other -isms would help advance the polarized national discourse.

WHAT IS RADICAL

To tie the pieces of this chapter into a whole, the common thread is the question of what is radical, meaning what will really make a difference. SJ purity can be seductive and appear more radical – but only because it is louder and more absolute. It is my contention that actually listening is one of the best ways to achieve justice in the world, and thus is the most radical. The simple reason is that marginalized people tend to be voiceless in their position in society, and being listened to gives one a voice.

What if we all could resist jumping to making demands and assigning blame, and instead could accept discomfort and be open to change? Or, another way to ask that question is to ask what conditions would make it feel safe to do that? For the incident in the office with personal space violation, the volunteers felt violated to the point of being unsafe, and when anyone is feeling that kind of danger, they can have a reflex action to protect themselves and make a barrier against sharing feelings and against listening deeply.

A safe space for vulnerable growth is not safe just because someone has simply declared it a "safe space." A space is only safe when constant maintenance is done. That main-tenance involves regular listening and accepting differ-ences without judgment. Agora has felt extremely safe for most people, because of the leadership model that prac-tices among each other the same things we practice with callers.

The SJ movement appears to be a lot more about talking than listening, about aggression instead of compassion. It does not mix well with making spaces feel safe for growth.

Fun

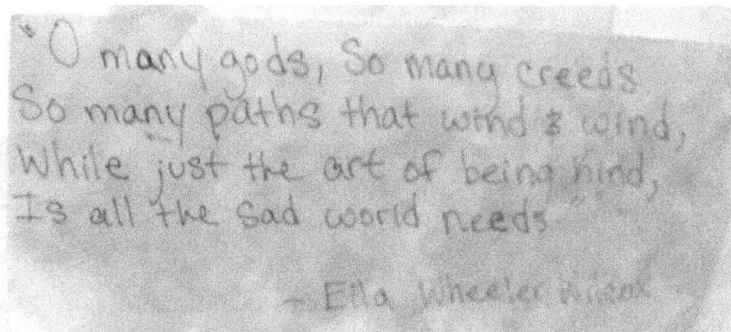

"O many gods, So many creeds,
So many paths that wind & wind,
While just the art of being kind,
Is all the sad world needs."

— Ella Wheeler Wilcox

COMMUNITY

Agora has an annual retreat away from the city. The first was in 1971 at Ghost Ranch, a landscape of cliffs and canyons in northern New Mexico. Molly insists it is just for fun and to give back to the volunteers, but she does not miss an opportunity for an educational growth experience. Saying it is "just" fun would be minimizing the vital role of fun and the connection to the wider purpose of this community.

In some college-age gatherings, there is quite a lot of social competition, with more attempts to be heard than to hear, resulting in one-upping each other's size of presence in an uproar of boastfulness. At the opposite end of that spectrum, when a lot of people who are predisposed to listening come together, there is a critical mass of sensitivity that quiets the space. People are more worried about being too centered rather than being left out, so they step it down and widen the circle, leaving the middle open. Agora retreats are like this. A giggle passes through the room; the slightest unease is noticed and held. For me, I experienced it as a heart bonding with everyone in a way that provided so much safety that it opened sides of me that I did not expect to see.

When we talk to callers who are doubting their chances of finding love, or who say they are unworthy or dumb, we do not contradict them with false reassurances that they are "fine" or that things will work out. We allow for negatives to have space. Like everyone, I carry around self doubt, which in most environments is unwelcome and thus I do not get a chance to express it and see it held by others. Without expression it lingers as the same self doubt for a long time. But at the Agora retreats, anything that comes out is carried through the room like ripples in a pond, with all of us being the water that the energy moves through. That input could be a confident comment, a joke, or a faltering sense of not being creative enough. Regardless of whether it is normally seen as a good or a bad thing, it ripples because it is okay to feel anything you feel.

Social-emotional pressure can go both ways. At a competitive gathering, even if it is fun, there is pressure towards me and I have to resist or push back; at a sensitive gathering, the pressure is reversed like a vacuum and the things in me are drawn out.

The circles-of-influence model at the core of the whole organization plays out in real time here, and to some extent also wherever a few Agorans are in the same place. That model is about giving: from the leadership to the next wider circle, to the next wider circle, and so on. I believe this is what people really want when they say they are seeking a feeling of "community."

Volunteer of the Month:

Stephanie

How did you decide to get involved with Agora?
During my freshman year of college at UNM I wo
Women's Resource Center and then became invol
Residence Life and Student Housing. Both of thes
always mentioned their love for the work that Ago
In the following year, as a Resident Advisor, I quic
that the part of the job I loved the most was being t
students when they were in crisis or just needed to
years of waiting for my schedule to allow it, I finally
_____ this summer. I have already met so many
_____ passion for helping those in th

Ellie is just the absolute kindest and most understanding individual I've had the pleasure of meeting. She is so supportive as a shift supervisor. I am beyond grateful to have her on my side when I'm taking calls."

"Hannah! I am so
that you are sitt
with us on W
You have
energy ab
stories
wond

Zoingo. I love sitting shift with you. You brighten the
Center by just being here!

"Thanks John R. for all of your help and support. You're
the best shift partner a person could ask for!"

"Thanks for cutting these green papers up Alex." - Riley

"Houston, Supreme queen. You are the greatest. I'm
always happy to be on shift with you!"

"Ellie, thank you so much for helping me with my first
call!! I really appreciate all the encouragement!!"

"John. Thanks for being s_
bein_

When volunteers have compassion fatigue, the retreats can help release that and recharge people. To me, there is no strict line between what is fun and what is therapeutic.

Throughout the book are some pictures of signs in the office. Instead of goals, org-charts, and performance charts, there are inspirations, thank-yous, and other celebrations of the Agorans. People add to these over the years.

We also have "volunteer of the month" interviews and "shout-outs" to enthusiastically celebrate all the contributions.

RETREAT THEMES

Molly builds the retreats around a theme with an extended art project, and adds games, ghost stories, and other old-fashioned fun. The art themes can be quite powerful because everyone is working from the same prompt, sharing ideas, and at the end we see the range of creativity and get a glimpse into each participant's process and story that they made into physical form. Here are some of the themes:

- **Roles**: Think about roles you hold in your life. Make masks that show one or more of these roles.

- **Balance**: Think about how to balance different parts of your life. Make hanging mobiles representing that balance.

- **Community**: Think about how we fit together. Decorate puzzle pieces representing that, and put the large puzzle together at the end.

- **Journeys**: Think about where you are going in life and what you need to take with you. Make and decorate boxes representing what you carry.

The rest of the chapter includes some of the community building and sometimes goofy games. These games are in the genre of "New Games" – a book from 1976 that explains many non-competitive games and challenges.

CONTINUUM

The leader calls out two opposites, like "book or magazine," or "summer or winter." Participants arrange themselves in a line representing the continuum between the opposites. People can ask and share why they have put themselves in a certain place. Some groups may want to add political or very personal opposites if people are ready to be put on the spot.

ZOOM

This game requires a pre-printed deck of cards – search the web for the phrase "Zoom/Re-Zoom" to find one. The cards start with a wide angle image, then include increasingly magnified images in the series. One image might be a person reading a book with a picture of a house on one page. The next card could be a zoom-in of the house with a person and his dog sitting outside. The next one might zoom in on the person and dog, showing a detail on the shirt, which leads to the next card, and so on.

The task is to hand the cards out at random, and then sort the group by the series of the cards. However, do not show your card to others; just mix in the group and verbally explain your card to others to find the person holding the card that is adjacent to yours.

A discussion on perspective-taking could follow. What was the most unexpected challenge?

HELIUM STICK

This cooperation game only works when a group really tunes into itself and no one is dominant. Use a yardstick or similar lightweight rod. Six people (three on each side) start by holding the yardstick up with one finger each. The task is to lower the yardstick to the ground gradually while maintaining the level, without anyone losing contact. The complicated part is to avoid too much force, which causes the stick to rise like helium.

A discussion on dominance could follow. Did you have to dial down or up?

ROPE SHAPES

Using a 50-foot rope for a group of 25, tie the ends together to make a loop, and arrange everyone equally around the loop, holding up the rope. The leader calls out a shape, such as a square. Without talking, the group must form a perfect square. Someone who self-nominates to be a corner might have to give up that position to make the sides equal.

After doing a square, try a triangle, infinity sign, or five-pointed star.

A discussion on leadership could follow. How did the group decide whom to follow, and were you a leader?

HUMAN KNOT

Form a circle with a group of about eight. Reach in one hand and take the hand of anyone else. Reach in the other hand and take the hand of anyone other than the first connection. Never let go of the hands. The task is to untangle the knot you have just created. You may have to step over and under arms but do not let go.

The game provides physical contact and builds cohesion in group problem solving.

THUMB BALL

This is a low-stakes introductions game. Using a soccer ball, write abbreviated get-to-know-you prompts in marker in each white pentagon or hexagon. Here are some ideas for prompts:

- First memory
- Embarrassment in elementary school
- A time when you were lost

- Worst kitchen disaster

- Missed opportunity

Toss the ball around the group. The catcher must answer the prompt under her or his right thumb at the time of the catch. Throw to everyone without repeating people.

PASS THE HOOP

Hold hands in a large circle. Using a hula hoop hanging from the starting person's arm, cause the hoop to pass around the circle without breaking the handholds. You must help your neighbor for this to work.

A variant uses a balloon held between your chin and chest, and passing it around without using hands.

LOOKING FOR

The group assembles on one side of the space except the first person to be It. That person says, "I'm looking for someone who ____" using a quality that is true about themselves. Examples could be the youngest sibling, born in another country, allergic to tomatoes, and so on. The first person to say "me!" goes to the opposite side and is It for the next round. Continue until everyone has found something in common and everyone has gone to the opposite side.

Now what?

FUTURE OF AGORA

Many callers try Agora first because they get the best results. Its positive effect is simply unquantifiable. Yet in 2022 the money is shifting away from us and towards professional 988 call centers. Those centers come from a different mindset – accountability and efficiency. Agora could have gotten into that stream of funding if we hired a team of 24-hour clinicians and agreed to the short calls and other restrictions. But Molly would not do that, since it would mean giving up on the successful and proven central principles of human connection – listening instead of fixing.

Agora call volume has gone down because of these funding shifts, and Molly is retiring. I fear the sun may be setting on this organization's 52 years on a shoestring. The sad part for me is not as much about the life cycle of the partic-ular student club – it is more about the fading of Agora's durable principles into obscurity, and the fear that policy decisions will be made myopically with an adherence to unsubstantiated, politically popular values, or based on profit.

That is why this book exists, and why 50% of the earnings will go to volunteer crisis centers.

HOPES

The rest of this last chapter contains a summary of my hopes and recommendations for policy. These are given to you through me, but ultimately come from all the people in crisis that I have spoken with. These do not come from research or other sources, but just an organized restatement of what so many people have told me they need to be able to move through their crises.

UNDERSTANDING FACTORS OF CRISIS IN THE CULTURE

The hopes in this section are things people in crisis want us all to understand, and what we need to understand to move beyond myopic policies. Broad understanding of these topics could help alleviate the severity of emotional trauma in the first place, and thus prevent crises from escalating.

1. Understand that children are already complete

Children have 100% of the spirit and feelings of anyone else. All ages of people need direction, teaching, community, and contribution. It is harmful for children to be treated as if they are empty, un-formed, or irrelevant.

2. Understand that the work of the soul is more important than being happy

Any true expression of feelings, whether it is happiness, anger, sadness, or fear, helps us move forward. We do not need "toxic positivity," or the unhealthy social pressure to appear and act happy all the time. Behaviorism, a cousin of positivity, focuses too much on the externals and ignores trauma and opportunities for growth from within. Ignoring the soul can lead to trauma.

Being versed in having a successful bad day is a huge benefit and inoculation against escalating crisis. Children need modeling about and permission for having bad days, while being honest with feelings.

3. Understand white supremacy

White supremacy is wider than overt racism; it is all the assumptions about who is legitimate and who is the "other" that pervade culture and institutions. The dismissing and fighting ways to think about discrimination are both divisive, though opposites. Progressive ideas like staying in your lane and being an ally to an oppressed group can perpetuate othering. Marginalizing is a source of trauma, and any kind of othering interferes with the ability of the community and systems to help.

More generally, any form of stratification can have the effect of traumatizing the marginalized, individually and as a collective trauma.

4. Understand the danger of achievement-oriented culture

Some cultures believe babies are gifts from the divine, whose contributions are gradually revealed as they grow up. But in the US, raising children has become an increasingly competitive sport where (in the extreme) children are channeled into achieving milestones, as if they are empty vessels who would do nothing of value without external incentives. The starting point of being accepted only for achievements instead of loved unconditionally sets the stage for a lifetime of trauma.

When love or respect are conditionally based on achievement, our foundational esteem becomes less solid, and this can be an element of crisis. Being called a failure can be self-fulfilling.

5. Understand education quality over quantity

Education policy, which appears to be controlled by the criminally uninformed, often stresses quantity over quality, resulting in a stream of dangerous proposals for longer school days and earlier testable academic work. When put in place, we see four and five-year-olds sitting for hours doing so-called "skill building" worksheets. This form of imprisonment crushes the life force. We must stop this and let children play, as play is the work of being a child.

Primary education works because of relationships and one's natural curiosity being activated by meaningful people. It does not work because of the test scores, the hours spent on a topic, or other more easily measured outcomes. Subjecting students to tedious and invasive levels of schooling that interfere with a private life can contribute to crisis. In particular during the pandemic, the meaninglessness of schooling came to the surface for many.

6. Understand us/them thinking in nonprofits and healthcare

Othering can be so ubiquitous in our institutions that we cannot see it clearly. In mental health and charities, the split between providers and those being served can interfere with autonomy, especially if the recipient is judged to be incompetent or dysfunctional. This dynamic can repel people from crisis care, shelters, or other services.

7. Understand bullying

Anti-bullying initiatives that primarily target bullies in school rather than their victims are doomed from the start; people do not give up power because you ask nicely. Bullying only stops when power differences are evened out. One of the largest areas of bullying that we willfully ignore is bullying by adults. Victims of bullying lose autonomy, and that situation can lead to crisis. The shift that should occur is towards positive safety – that is, respecting autonomy with community peer support (safety in numbers) in ways that actually even out the power differences.

8. Understand the effect of social media

Social media use has been linked to greater isolation and extremism. Relationships on-line may be between two constructed personas, using posed and digitally altered pictures. These personas compete for attention in spaces starved of actual community, where social ranking is made explicit. Older people need to understand that on-line life is real and consequential; simply unplugging is not a realistic option.

When we have options to meet for friendship and dating in traditional off-line ways, seeing all the blemishes of real people, we are more likely to be part of a durable support network. A network is key to successfully navigating a crisis.

9. Understand safe spaces

Safe spaces must be maintained through continuous supportive communication, not just declared by a good intention. For some people, most places feel dangerous, even those declared "safe." Having a place that really feels safe to open up in and be authentic can mitigate crisis.

10. Understand the limits of social justice ideology

The rigid ideology of part of the social justice (SJ) movement can act as a barrier to compassionate listening, because ideology does not tolerate dissent.

Being triggered is not a sign of a violation; in fact it can be part of healing.

Shunning, canceling, or anything that chills authentic communication or divides a community also threatens listening as a mode of healing.

GOVERNMENT POLICY

The hopes in this section relate to tangible policies that could be made by governments.

11. Eliminate profit interests in health, counseling, and crisis response

Market systems are essential in a free, democratic society, but they are not the only way to channel incentives into action. In particular, the fields of health and education draw people largely because of our natural motive to care for others, rather than to get rich. All those people whose personal motives are coming from the right place should be working in organizations that elevate those values, such that organizational structures are furthering the values of the people working in the organizations. Without that, the profit motive may reduce quality to a minimum measurable standard.

12. Address housing and poverty

Threats of homelessness are a common cause of crisis. This is sometimes due to individuals or couples simply not being able to make it in the economy, and sometimes it also has to do with young people being evicted by parents, or non-working women being kicked out by partners. Or vulnerable people may be forced to live in unhealthy conditions because it is the only option. Those with disabilities can be at even higher risk of these situations due to lack of income.

So-called "housing-first" policies are based on the understanding that people cannot effectively take care of mental health issues, education, food, etc., if they have no place to live. This approach should be spread widely.

Going further, a policy of guaranteed minimum income could go a long way to solving a lot of crisis factors, because it retrains recipients' autonomy more than a patchwork of programs that target food, housing, health, and transportation separately.

13. Give financial help in transitions

It costs more to move than to stay put. For some, a crisis calls for a change, which can be a move or education, or something that costs more than doing nothing.

So in addition to basic income, some people need more help during a crisis. In some cases where the police check on someone in person, it may be more effective and less costly to just hand the person 500 dollars and drive away, rather than to take them to a hospital or try to involve themselves in solving the root problems.

This kind of policy may feel wrong, like a band-aid approach. But imagine yourself in the situation and needing to increase your autonomy. Having an immediate range of choices about how to manage the crisis would allow someone to get a motel room to distance themselves from an abuser, or get a new phone, or pay to board their dog (pets are a lifeline for many). These solutions are things that a system cannot come up with generically, as they are specific to each person. Money empowers. (The suggestion about 500 dollars is perhaps not practical as I have written it, but that is how we need to be thinking about crisis.)

14. Make gun ownership orderly

Given that guns account for a large part of suicides, any way to reduce the number or availability of them could help. Specific policies are outside the scope of this book, but the situation today in the US is dangerous: young people can get guns in an untracked manner, quickly and without training, allowing them to act abruptly on rage. Gun ownership, being protected by the Constitution, cannot be eliminated, but it should be a process that is more deliberate, measured, traceable, and educational.

To be extra clear, the thrust of this recommendation is not to make it impossible to suicide with a gun, but to reduce the number of suicides done rashly during a poor state of judgment, especially by young males.

15. Build settlements with community in mind

Community-oriented design of towns and cities can help ease isolation. Examples of improvements are mixed-use neighborhoods rather than suburban sprawl, more transit access, more walking connections, and more visibility to public space. Smaller towns or so-called "village centers" within cities can build communities where people know each other, yielding better support networks.

Lack of transportation is an isolating factor that prevents people from solving their own problems, including the problem of isolation. Many cities outside North America prove that transportation can be made universal.

16. Allow for assisted suicide

For people with terminal illnesses, and possibly for others, dying with dignity on their own terms is often not allowed. People mostly want to solve a crisis and become stronger, but when many years have passed without a reprieve in the pain, it could be time to allow life to end. The same principles of ensuring that people retain their autonomy and have a community support network apply both to crisis resolution and to assisted suicide. We should not make it so difficult to die that people are forced to do it secretly or rashly, and cause an upheaval in their families.

INSTITUTIONAL POLICIES

The hopes in this section relate to tangible policies that could be made by schools, businesses, and non-governmental organizations.

17. Implement data-supported youth safety

The US has maniacally constructed a fortress of "safety" around youth in a way that appears uninformed of actual safety threats and is demeaning and limiting to children, making them feel imprisoned. Perhaps the most egregious fantasy is the thought that fences, gates, and surveillance around schools keeps dangers out, when in fact, many of the dangers to children are the people who work inside those walls. Higher visibility in public space and youth spaces, with more routes of egress, is more likely to yield safety, while also allowing youth to grow more independence. In any case, the policies need to be based on data rather than fear.

Parents who keep watch over the communications and every movement of their children may unwittingly be contributing to crisis situations for them.

The farmer who builds stronger walls to keep the fox out of the henhouse is acting rationally. But that situation is not parallel to human safety because the fox does not have the key to the henhouse. In our case, it is different because we do not know *a priori* who is a danger and who has the keys.

18. Build opportunities for relevance outside the workforce

Teens and retired people need to contribute to society in some way, regardless of money. It may be paid or not, but in any case, we need to build capacity in all our institutions to support working for reasons other than basic profitability or "economic productivity." When people feel irrelevant, they can be stuck in a crisis.

19. Throw a wrench in the nonprofit racket

The "nonprofit racket" is the game of seeking grant-funded projects, then using the money to bait people into participation, then measure success by multiplying out the number of people caught by the number of hours spent. Not all nonprofits work this way, but it appears to be a common incentive pattern. It could affect community health services if the unmeasurable outcomes of healing from trauma are judged to be less important than some other numerical result.

This hope echoes the hope above that health and crisis response would be free of profit interests. A similar problem exists throughout the nonprofit world and it also has to be addressed there.

20. Develop community standards for social media

Unchecked, social media companies will maximize advertising revenue by rewarding addictive behavior while tracking and profiting from personal information. A balance of power can be better achieved through certain transparency and fair-use laws (as currently exist in certain forms in California and Europe), and by advancing the organizations that promote ethical internet standards. It is impossible to outlaw dehumanizing motivations in a market economy, but we can organize for improvements.

21. Hold a national depolarization dialog

With political polarization at an unusual high, both progressive and conservative ideologies are more rigid, and more people are believing that the other side is composed of demons (figuratively or sometimes literally) without ever talking with them. Along with social media and other factors, a decline in community dialog could be fueling a decline in overall listening skills and the ability to accept significant differences in other people.

A large-scale organized way to hold dialogs could help with these problems, and help with certain crisis situations that are connected to political hate.

MENTAL HEALTH SYSTEMS

The hopes in this section are about how mental health systems can better serve people in crisis.

22. Blur the lines between healing modes and social classes

Social service systems have a tendency to organize along Maslow's hierarchy of needs (presented in the Learning chapter), in the sense that the "basic" needs need to be met first before it makes sense to start on higher needs on the pyramid. But related research (and common sense) has shown that people will sometimes give up food and shelter more easily than they will give up belonging. Indeed, crisis is rarely just about basic needs being unmet; it is often about the social and spiritual needs being unmet.

Services in the US are glaringly segregated by class. The low end of services, which are responsible for food and housing, may overly control and infantilize recipients, while at the opposite end, wealthy people pay therapists out of pocket for help with being present and bringing their chakras into harmony.

But all people deserve all of these levels, and the higher levels should not be denied to those who have not obtained the lower levels. The more multidisciplinary awareness and blurring the lines there can be, the more gaps in the system could be filled, and the less othering might occur.

23. Embrace Freudian tradition, not just coping

As with building a house or getting a work assignment done, often a quick fix or practical shortcut is easier and cheaper, but does not last or does not support the next steps well. I see a lot of the coping-focused therapy that people get these days to be practical but temporary like that. Therapy in the Freudian tradition is longer, messier, and has more risks and more rewards.

On the question of when we should allow or direct a conversation to go into someone's ancient traumas, it is not answered in the abstract: in other words, we should not go there or avoid going there as a rule, but only go there if the current crisis necessitates it. So we should definitely dig up the distant past if that is where the answer to the current problem is buried. That way, we are always staying in present feelings and needs, and not going off digging up stuff based on a theory.

24. Measure hospitalization and psychiatric outcomes by patient

Psychiatric hospitals need to be patient-centered in the whole way they handle funding, measure success, and make changes from feedback. Currently, doctor's evaluation of success is counted too strongly over that of the patients. When huge numbers of patients say that the hospital experience was traumatic, that needs to inform a change.

25. Develop masculine-aware alternatives

Recall the story of men effectively helping each other in a very masculine way, which is not a standard form of therapeutic interaction (see the Categories chapter).

The bro energy that does not directly talk about feelings seems to be vital for some people because it is supportive and works with some common male issues of honor, power, and honing rage into action. I do not believe we necessarily need a different crisis line or a different way to talk to men. I think that some men can use the crisis lines effectively as they are, but that some people also need something that is a completely different format to fill the gap. Remember that most people who take their life are male, and they mostly do not reach out for help in the form of talking in those final moments. The gap there is fatal.

What would that format be? It has to involve more physical things and less talk. We should not pressure men to work with feelings only in the way that women usually find works better. It has to allow people to demonstrate their skills, strengths, achievements and knowledge, without minimizing that drive to achieve. Some people need a place where they can confess to their own transgressions in complete guaranteed safety, especially about sexual acts or anything else taboo, which cannot be safely discussed anywhere else and would be harder to admit to a female listener.

The image I have in mind is a hunting trip with vast physical space and lots of time. This is not practical as a systematic response to crisis, but something that has some of those elements might be practical.

26. Expand mid-range intensity options

The health system in general suffers from a gap in the mid range. If you have a small health complaint, you can wait weeks or months to see a doctor on their schedule. At the other extreme, if you are bleeding to death, you can go to the ER. But what if the problem is medium – too big to wait for a doctor appointment, but too small for the ER? The category of "urgent care" was popularized in the 1980s and addresses that gap somewhat. Anecdotally, urgent care can suffer from all the limitations of both extremes, and many people with those medium health conditions in the US do not get the level of care that they would in a country with a true national health system.

For mental health, especially in acute crisis, the gap is giant. People can go to inpatient psychiatric hospitals for a complete upheaval of life and massive costs, or they could wait days, weeks, or more for a therapist. Crisis lines exist in that gap but we need so much more capacity and many more options.

Some of these mid range options are as follows:

- Crisis lines with low waiting times.

- Free or low cost counseling, scheduled within one week.

- Crisis stabilization units, with beds like a shelter, but for mental health stabilization.

- Mobile outreach teams, which can have social workers coordinating with police, and can respond via calls to 988 or 911.

- Rape crisis centers with enough capacity for same day admitting.

- Facilitated support groups, particularly for rape survivors and those with substance addictions.

27. Forget artificial intelligence

Some observers have promoted therapies and crisis response powered by artificial intelligence (AI, or "bots"), due to the profit potential, and the fact that the demand for low-cost therapy is greater than the supply of therapists. For people in deep crisis, this type of intervention would be a cruel joke, for reasons listed throughout this book. No matter how good the computer's logic may become, the relationship matters, and people can feel it when something touches the other person. As of this writing, the best AI powered conversations are somewhat hard to detect and the computer could definitely say some insightful and helpful things. But the bot would not be affected by the caller. I have cried along with callers, and they change me, but a computer could only fake-feel something. Once a caller realizes it is in fact a bot, the sudden sense of being alone could make the whole experience ineffective or negative.

On text, occasionally someone is convinced that we are bots, and to their point, it is true that the second and third responses from a counselor are often similar – things like: "I'm so sorry you're going through that. Tell me more." Only one person has actually disconnected under the belief that I was a bot, but everyone else who asked about that has felt the truth of it after we get past those initial few lines of dialog.

I still believe there can be a role for AI. Consider language learning, or any other subject that is amenable to flash cards or other rote methods for at least part of the learning process. Computer instruction can work well in those cases. There are programs of instruction that an AI-enhanced software teacher could lead you through, which could include calming techniques, meditation, and other exercises. It does not appear to me that a crisis is the time to talk to a bot though.

Remember also that in the larger context of Agora, we are effective because of the totality of the training and circles of influence model. It does not exist solely to efficiently fix people; it is not a commodity. Tech companies who market AI systems are doing it for money, and are missing all of that context.

CRISIS RESPONSE POLICIES

The hopes in this section deal with specifics for crisis centers.

28. Use the circles model in an educational context

The circles model helps eliminate us/them thinking and prioritizes growth and education in listeners, leading to them being energized and committed. Many other reasons for this model's success have been listed in this book.

29. Fund nonjudgmental listening

We need to fund simply listening. It sounds free, but it is not. Professional leadership, training, materials and facilities are needed even if the listeners are volunteering. It is a lot less costly than other ways, but it is not free.

This really means we need to fund it separately from all other things, so that a crisis response organization can focus on listening and do that well.

30. Prioritize callers over data

I met someone out on a trail and I mentioned I did suicide counseling. She recounted a story of calling 988 and said they wanted so much information – name, address, call-back number, insurance, and so on – that she finally hung up on them before getting to talk about the reason for the call. The pressures of a professionalized system may make this way of starting an interaction seem reasonable, but we really need to step outside that mindset and imagine the experience of calling in to be greeted with a maze of a bureaucracy.

Volunteer lines like Agora are more likely to answer: "Hi, this is Cynthia." and that is it: A real person with an opening for a real, but short, relationship. The center of spiritual gravity needs to stay with the caller, while the energy on the counselor's end of the line is smaller and receptive from the start, not demanding.

To the extent we really need statistics, we can just estimate. The data are never so valuable that we should prioritize them over establishing genuine rapport.

31. Do not triage or screen calls

Because people in crisis cannot always access their full capacity for judgment or communication, they would not always be able to say what level of crisis they are in. For example, a person may have developed a mechanism of saying "I'm fine" under duress because of past abuse. Therefore no matter how innocuous or unproductive a call may seem at first, it is essential to try to stretch it out to at least ten minutes or so in order to determine the real level of distress. Even when it really turns out to be a chat about nothing in particular with someone who was just lonely, that is also important: isolation is a problem which a listening service can help with.

Another reason it is counterproductive to ask screening questions is that it feels judgmental. With that approach, the call does not start out with the more important phase of building rapport; it starts out with the caller being forced to prove they have a legitimate need.

32. Allow frequent callers

Some people have needed to call crisis lines day after day with no apparent change in their situation. Mostly, these are people who do not have regular contact with family or neighbors and are looking for a daily dose of connection with someone, or they may be in an extended crisis. Agora allows for this, although we put a time limit on some people. It is important to honor the needs of everyone, and our society can afford to do this, so we should.

Also consider the practicality and cost-effectiveness of preventative care in general: usually prevention of any problem (disease, crisis, homelessness, car crashes, etc.) is cheaper than addressing the aftermath of the problem. Frequent contact is a form of crisis prevention.

33. Always augment autonomy

As discussed earlier, one of the common factors in any kind of life crisis is lack of autonomy. When people in crisis (who may be hypervigilant about threats to their autonomy) are told what to do at every turn, it makes the crisis worse. For some, the experience of being taken against their will by police or medical people and then locked in a hospital is the worst event in their life, worse than all the precipitating factors of the crisis. Of course if there is a verifiable threat to life, it may be necessary to detain someone, but much of the time there is no basis for a sudden loss of freedom.

So, whenever there is a choice, allow the person in crisis to determine the next step.

In an in-person crisis response situation, we need to think of these as a "kiosk style" of mental health services – think like Lucy's 5 cent psychiatric booth in Peanuts. A kiosk has no walls and no presumption that the customer has to stay for any certain length of time. People need the freedom to leave the moment the services are not helping, or if they simply change their mind.

Those kiosk style services could include consideration of some autonomy-augmenting solution other than traditional inpatient or outpatient care. For example, money for a motel room, or some other offering that is not directly a mental health service, can give the person more choices to steer their way through the crisis. In that way it is indirectly a mental health service.

34. Use part-time paraprofessional volunteers

Instead of untrained peer listeners or professional clinicians being the only options, the paraprofessional model of substantial non-degree training and evaluation (40 hours in the case of Agora) ensures that callers reach someone who is trained in listening, even if they are not trained in any area of psychology.

The listeners do not need to be volunteer, but the volunteer model allows for more people to be trained (which has the ripple effect of education helping the world in other ways), and for them to work fewer hours (which has the benefit of full engagement without burnout). Volunteer operations still need funding for professional leadership and office space, but the funding level is far less than for a team of paid professionals.

Ultimately this allows more people to respond to crisis, so there are short waiting periods, and they can talk longer. Callers can approach it with a different expectation, knowing that it is a nonprofessional counselor on the line.

35. Allow for anonymity and confidentiality (adults)

Phone and text-based help has the built in advantage of allowing people to stay anonymous. A helper might feel the lack of trust is for invalid reasons, but it is always a valid reason in the mind of the caller. No one should be pressured to reveal identifying information.

Even in person, if we had universal care without the complexity of insurance, it should be possible for someone to receive inpatient care under a pseudonym. Certain mental health conditions come with the type of paranoia that can scare those persons away from treatment otherwise.

Given that anonymous in-person care may be a pipedream, it could be more practical to offer a choice. So as a person with a secret that needs to come out, you can choose a traditional option or a truly confidential option:

- The traditional option, with mandated reporting, would bring you into the system of care with all its features like insurance coverage and prescriptions, but it would be clear that they may not be completely confidential.

- The confidential option could be much more limited – basically a listening service that does not give referrals or advice, does not ask for a caller's name or location, does not have a low time limit, and does not collect data for statistics.

36. Develop a system for teens

Earlier I discussed the pros and cons of mandated reporting for minors – whether a counselor must report a threat of harm to oneself or others to parents or police.

The natural process of separation from parents does not happen instantly on a timer at the age of 18 – it is gradual. Thus the system of crisis response needs some gradations depending on age.

My sense is that below the age of 13, children should not be afforded secrecy because they lack the ability to make sound judgments about how to handle bad situations. For those children, the rules should stay the same; namely full parent involvement. The systems for investigating child neglect and abuse may be underfunded, but they appear to be based on the right principles.

The age range of 13-17 is where we have a major problem. For teens, their parents are often connected to the problems they are having and when they need to unload something, it is really important to them that it does not get back to the parents. Since teens know they cannot trust a school counselor in this way, they may turn to people in internet forums or other less safe options. As the mother of children whose safety I worried about in those years, I still believe they should have been able to tell other people things that they wished to keep away from me. And those other people should be trained and trustworthy, not just someone who gives them attention online.

Minor teens should have three options:

1. Resolve with their parents as the first approach (that is, the same model as for pre-teen children), but with high transparency and follow-through.

2. Use a fully confidential system with no mandated reporting, as suggested above for adults.

3. Access a third-party mediator, with conditional adult privileges. The mediator would make an assessment of their developmental level and whether parents are part of the problem, and then, based on that discretion, may allow the teen to access other mental health services as an adult. The third party could impose crisis reduction rules, such as allowing teens to have an unmonitored phone, if that is against the parents' wishes.

THE END

That is all of my 36 hopes. Let's do this!

9798987539903